D1436462

A
MIDSUMMER-NIGHT'S DREAM

BLACKIE & SON LIMITED
50 Old Bailey, LONDON
17 Stanhope Street, GLASGOW

BLACKIE & SON (INDIA) LIMITED
Warwick House, Fort Street, BOMBAY

BLACKIE & SON (CANADA) LIMITED
TORONTO

Titania. Thou art as wise as thou art beautiful.
(Act III, Scene 1.)

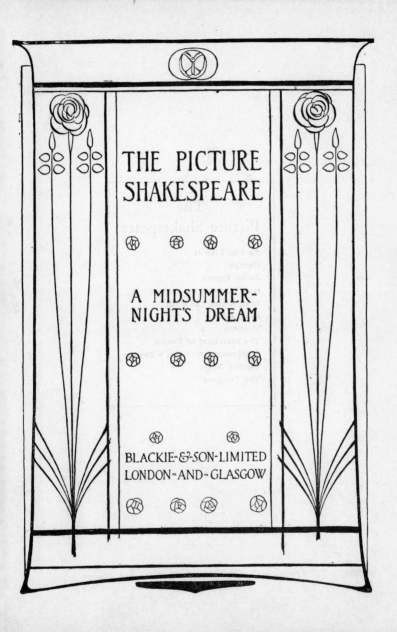

THE PICTURE SHAKESPEARE

A MIDSUMMER-NIGHT'S DREAM

BLACKIE · & · SON · LIMITED
LONDON · AND · GLASGOW

The Picture Shakespeare

As You Like It
Hamlet
Julius Cæsar
King Richard the Second
King Henry the Fifth
King John
Macbeth
The Merchant of Venice
A Midsummer-Night's Dream
Twelfth Night
The Tempest

Printed in Great Britain by Blackie & Son, Ltd., Glasgow

CONTENTS

CONTENTS

INTRODUCTION

THE STORY OF THE PLAY[1]

There was a law in the city of Athens which gave to its citizens the power of compelling their daughters to marry whomsoever they pleased: for upon a daughter's refusing to marry the man her father had chosen to be her husband, the father was empowered by this law to cause her to be put to death; but as fathers do not often desire the death of their own daughters, even though they do happen to prove a little refractory, this law was seldom or never put in execution, though perhaps the young ladies of that city were not unfrequently threatened by their parents with the terrors of it.

There was one instance, however, of an old man, whose name was Egeus, who actually did come before Theseus (at that time the reigning duke of Athens) to complain that his daughter Hermia, whom he had commanded to marry Demetrius, a young man of a noble Athenian family, refused to obey him because she loved another young Athenian named Lysander. Egeus demanded justice of Theseus, and desired that this cruel law might be put in force against his daughter.

Hermia pleaded in excuse for her disobedience that Demetrius had formerly professed love for her dear friend Helena, and that Helena loved Demetrius to distraction; but this honourable reason which Hermia gave for not obeying her father's command moved not the stern Egeus.

[1] From Charles Lamb's *Tales from Shakspeare.*

7

Theseus, though a great and merciful prince, had no power to alter the laws of his country; therefore he could only give Hermia four days to consider of it: and at the end of that time, if she still refused to marry Demetrius, she was to be put to death.

When Hermia was dismissed from the presence of the duke, she went to her lover Lysander, and told him the peril she was in, and that she must either give up him and marry Demetrius, or lose her life in four days.

Lysander was in great affliction at hearing these evil tidings; but recollecting that he had an aunt who lived at some distance from Athens, and that at the place where she lived the cruel law could not be put in force against Hermia (this law not extending beyond the boundaries of the city), he proposed to Hermia that she should steal out of her father's house that night, and go with him to his aunt's house, where he would marry her. "I will meet you", said Lysander, "in the wood a few miles without the city; in that delightful wood, where we have so often walked with Helena in the pleasant month of May."

To this proposal Hermia joyfully agreed; and she told no one of her intended flight but her friend Helena. Helena (as maidens will do foolish things for love) very ungenerously resolved to go and tell this to Demetrius, though she could hope no benefit from betraying her friend's secret, but the poor pleasure of following her faithless lover to the wood; for she well knew that Demetrius would go thither in pursuit of Hermia.

The wood in which Lysander and Hermia proposed to meet, was the favourite haunt of those little beings known by the name of *Fairies*.

Oberon the king, and Titania the queen, of the Fairies, with all their tiny train of followers, in this wood held their midnight revels.

Between this little king and queen of sprites there happened at this time a sad disagreement: they never met by moonlight in the shady walks of this pleasant wood but they were quarrelling, till all their fairy elves would creep into acorn-cups and hide themselves for fear.

The cause of this unhappy disagreement was Titania's refusing to give Oberon a little changeling boy, whose mother had been Titania's friend; and upon her death the fairy queen stole the child from its nurse and brought him up in the woods.

The night on which the lovers were to meet in this wood, as Titania was walking with some of her maids of honour, she met Oberon, attended by his train of fairy courtiers.

"Ill met by moonlight, proud Titania," said the airy king. The queen replied: "What, jealous Oberon, is it you? Fairies, skip hence; I have forsworn his company." "Tarry, rash fairy," said Oberon; "am not I thy lord? Why does Titania cross her Oberon? Give me your little changeling boy to be my page."

"Set your heart at rest," answered the queen; "your whole fairy kingdom buys not the boy of me." She then left her lord in great anger. "Well, go your way," said Oberon; "before the morning dawns I will torment you for this injury."

Oberon then sent for Puck, his chief favourite and privy councillor.

Puck (or, as he was sometimes called, Robin Good-fellow) was a shrewd and knavish sprite, and used to play comical pranks in the neighbouring villages; sometimes getting into the dairies and skimming the milk, sometimes plunging his light and airy form into the butter-churn, and while he was dancing his fantastic shape in the churn, in vain the dairy-maid would labour to change her cream into butter: nor had the village swains any better success; whenever Puck chose to play his freaks in the brewing copper, the ale was sure to be spoiled. When a few good neighbours were met to drink some

comfortable ale together, Puck would jump into the bowl
of ale in the likeness of a roasted crab, and when some
old goody was going to drink he would bob against her
lips and spill the ale over her withered chin; and presently
after, when the same old dame was gravely seating herself to tell her neighbours a sad and melancholy story,
Puck would slip her three-legged stool from under her,
and down toppled the poor old woman, and then the old
gossips would hold their sides and laugh at her, and
swear they never wasted a merrier hour.

"Come hither, Puck," said Oberon to this little merry
wanderer of the night; "fetch me the flower which maids
call *Love in Idleness*; the juice of that little purple flower
laid on the eyelids of those who sleep will make them,
when they awake, dote on the first thing they see. Some
of the juice of that flower I will drop on the eyelids of
my Titania when she is asleep; and the first thing she
looks upon when she opens her eyes she will fall in love
with, even though it be a lion, or a bear, a meddling
monkey, or a busy ape: and before I will take this charm
from off her sight, which I can do with another charm I
know of, I will make her give me that boy to be my page."

Puck, who loved mischief to his heart, was highly
diverted with this intended frolic of his master, and ran
to seek the flower; and while Oberon was waiting the
return of Puck, he observed Demetrius and Helena enter
the wood. He overheard Demetrius reproaching Helena
for following him, and after many unkind words on his
part, and gentle expostulations from Helena, reminding
him of his former love and professions of true faith to
her, he left her (as he said) to the mercy of the wild
beasts, and she ran after him as swiftly as she could.

The fairy king, who was always friendly to true
lovers, felt great compassion for Helena; and perhaps, as
Lysander said they used to walk by moonlight in this
pleasant wood, Oberon might have seen Helena in those

happy times when she was beloved by Demetrius. However that might be, when Puck returned with the little purple flower, Oberon said to his favourite, "Take a part of this flower: there has been a sweet Athenian lady here, who is in love with a disdainful youth; if you find him sleeping, drop some of the love-juice in his eyes, but contrive to do it when she is near him, that the first thing he sees when he awakes may be this despised lady. You will know the man by the Athenian garments which he wears." Puck promised to manage this matter very dextrously; and then Oberon went, unperceived by Titania, to her bower, where she was preparing to go to rest. Her fairy bower was a bank, where grew wild thyme, cowslips, and sweet violets under a canopy of woodbine, musk-roses, and eglantine. There Titania always slept some part of the night; her coverlet the enamelled skin of a snake, which, though a small mantle, was wide enough to wrap a fairy in.

He found Titania giving orders to her fairies how they were to employ themselves while she slept. "Some of you", said her majesty, "must kill cankers in the musk-rose buds, and some wage war with the bats for their leathern wings, to make my small elves coats; and some of you keep watch that the clamorous owl, that nightly hoots, come not near me; but first sing me to sleep." Then they began to sing this song:—

'You spotted snakes with double tongue,
   Thorny hedgehogs, be not seen;
Newts and blind-worms, do no wrong,
   Come not near our Fairy Queen.
      Philomel, with melody
      Sing in our sweet lullaby,
Lulla, lulla, lullaby, lulla, lulla, lullaby:
      Never harm,
      Nor spell, nor charm,
   Come our lovely lady nigh;
   So good-night, with lullaby."

When the fairies had sung their queen asleep with this pretty lullaby, they left her, to perform the important services she had enjoined them. Oberon then softly drew near his Titania, and dropped some of the love-juice on her eyelids, saying:

> "What thou seest, when thou dost wake,
>   Do it for thy true-love sake".

But to return to Hermia, who made her escape out of her father's house that night, to avoid the death she was doomed to for refusing to marry Demetrius. When she entered the wood, she found her dear Lysander waiting for her, to conduct her to his aunt's house; but before they had passed half through the wood, Hermia was so much fatigued that Lysander, who was very careful of this dear lady, who had proved her affection for him even by hazarding her life for his sake, persuaded her to rest till morning on a bank of soft moss, and lying down himself on the ground at some little distance, they soon fell fast asleep. Here they were found by Puck, who, seeing a handsome young man asleep, and perceiving that his clothes were made in the Athenian fashion, and that a pretty lady was sleeping near him, concluded that this must be the Athenian maid and her disdainful lover whom Oberon had sent him to seek; and he naturally enough conjectured that, as they were alone together, she must be the first thing he would see when he awoke: so without more ado he proceeded to pour some of the juice of the little purple flower into his eyes. But it so fell out that Helena came that way, and, instead of Hermia, was the first object Lysander beheld when he opened his eyes: and, strange to relate, so powerful was the love-charm, all his love for Hermia vanished away, and Lysander fell in love with Helena.

Had he first seen Hermia when he awoke, the blunder Puck committed would have been of no consequence, for he could not love that faithful lady too well; but for poor Lysander to be forced by a fairy love-charm to forget his own true Hermia, and to run after another lady and leave Hermia asleep quite alone in a wood at midnight, was a sad chance indeed.

Thus this misfortune happened. Helena, as has been before related, endeavoured to keep pace with Demetrius when he ran away so rudely from her; but she could not continue this unequal race long, men being always better runners in a long race than ladies. Helena soon lost sight of Demetrius; and as she was wandering about, dejected and forlorn, she arrived at the place where Lysander was sleeping. "Ah!" said she, "this is Lysander lying on the ground: is he dead or asleep?" Then gently touching him, she said: "Good sir, if you are alive, awake". Upon this Lysander opened his eyes, and (the love-charm beginning to work) immediately addressed her in terms of extravagant love and admiration; telling her she as much excelled Hermia in beauty as a dove does a raven, and that he would run through fire for her sweet sake; and many more such lover-like speeches. Helena, knowing Lysander was her friend Hermia's lover, and that he was solemnly engaged to marry her, was in the utmost rage when she heard herself addressed in this manner; for she thought (as well she might) that Lysander was making a jest of her. "Oh!" said she, "why was I born to be mocked and scorned by everyone? Is it not enough, is it not enough, young man, that I can never get a sweet look or a kind word from Demetrius; but you, sir, must pretend in this disdainful manner to court me? I thought, Lysander, you were a lord of more true gentleness." Saying these words in great anger, she ran away; and Lysander followed her, quite forgetful of his own Hermia, who was still asleep.

When Hermia awoke, she was in a sad fright at find-

ing herself alone. She wandered about the wood, not
knowing what was become of Lysander, or which way
to go to seek for him. In the meantime Demetrius, not
being able to find Hermia and his rival Lysander, and
fatigued with his fruitless search, was observed by Oberon
fast asleep. Oberon had learnt by some questions he had
asked of Puck that he had applied the love-charm to the
wrong person's eyes; and now, having found the person
first intended, he touched the eyelids of the sleeping
Demetrius with the love juice, and he instantly awoke;
and the first thing he saw being Helena, he, as Lysander
had done before, began to address love-speeches to her:
and just at that moment Lysander, followed by Hermia
(for through Puck's unlucky mistake it was now become
Hermia's turn to run after her lover), made his appearance; and then Lysander and Demetrius, both speaking
together, made love to Helena, they being each one under
the influence of the same potent charm.

The astonished Helena thought that Demetrius, Lysander, and her once dear friend Hermia were all in a plot
together to make a jest of her.

Hermia was as much surprised as Helena: she knew not
why Lysander and Demetrius, who both before loved her,
were now become the lovers of Helena; and to Hermia the
matter seemed to be no jest.

The ladies, who before had always been the dearest of
friends, now fell to high words together.

"Unkind Hermia," said Helena, "it is you have set
Lysander on, to vex me with mock praises; and your other
lover Demetrius, who used almost to spurn me with his
foot, have you not bid him call me Goddess, Nymph, rare,
precious, and celestial? He would not speak thus to me,
whom he hates, if you did not set him on to make a jest of
me. Unkind Hermia, to join with men in scorning your
poor friend. Have you forgot our school-day friendship?
How often, Hermia, have we two, sitting on one cushion,

both singing one song, with our needles working the same flower, both on the same sampler wrought; growing up together in fashion of a double cherry, scarcely seeming parted?   Hermia, it is not friendly in you, it is not maidenly, to join with men in scorning your poor friend."

"I am amazed at your passionate words," said Hermia: "I scorn you not; it seems you scorn me."   "Ay, do," returned Helena, "persevere, counterfeit serious looks, and make mouths at me when I turn my back; then wink at each other, and hold the sweet jest up.   If you had any pity, grace, or manners, you would not use me thus."

While Helena and Hermia were speaking these angry words to each other, Demetrius and Lysander left them, to fight together in the wood for the love of Helena.

When they found the gentlemen had left them, they departed, and once more wandered weary in the wood in search of their lovers.

As soon as they were gone, the fairy king, who with little Puck had been listening to their quarrels, said to him, "This is your negligence, Puck; or did you do this wilfully?"   "Believe me, king of shadows," answered Puck, "it was a mistake: did not you tell me I should know the man by his Athenian garments?   However, I am not sorry this has happened, for I think their jangling makes me excellent sport."   "You heard", said Oberon, "that Demetrius and Lysander are gone to seek a convenient place to fight in.   I command you to overhang the night with a thick fog, and lead these quarrelsome lovers so astray in the dark that they shall not be able to find each other.   Counterfeit each of their voices to the other, and with bitter taunts provoke them to follow you, while they think it is their rival's tongue they hear.   See you do this, till they are so weary that they can go no farther; and when you find they are asleep, drop the juice of this other flower into Lysander's eyes, and when he awakes he will forget his new love for Helena, and return to his old passion for Hermia; and then the two fair ladies may each one be happy with the man she loves; and they will think all that has passed a vexatious dream. About this quickly, Puck; and I will go and see what sweet love my Titania has found."

Titania was still sleeping, and Oberon seeing a clown near her, who had lost his way in the wood, and was like-wise asleep: "This fellow", said he, "shall be my Titania's true-love"; and clapping an ass's head over the clown's, it seemed to fit him as well as if it had grown upon his own shoulders. Though Oberon fixed the ass's head on very gently, it awakened him, and rising up, unconscious of what Oberon had done to him, he went towards the bower where the fairy queen slept.

"Ah! what angel is that I see?" said Titania, opening her eyes, and the juice of the little purple flower beginning to take effect: "Are you as wise as you are beautiful?"

"Why, mistress," said the foolish clown, "if I have wit enough to find the way out of this wood, I have enough to serve my turn."

"Out of the wood do not desire to go," said the en-amoured queen. "I am a spirit of no common rate. I love you. Go with me, and I will give you fairies to attend upon you."

She then called four of her fairies: their names were Pease-blossom, Cobweb, Moth, and Mustard-seed.

"Attend", said the queen, "upon this sweet gentleman: hop in his walks, and gambol in his sight; feed him with grapes and apricots, and steal for him the honey-bags from the bees. Come, sit with me," said she to the clown, "and let me play with your amiable hairy cheeks, my beautiful ass! and kiss your fair large ears, my gentle joy!"

"Where is Pease-blossom?" said the ass-headed clown, not much regarding the fairy queen's courtship, but very proud of his new attendants.

(B 465)

"Here, sir," said little Pease-blossom.

"Scratch my head," said the clown. "Where is Cob web?"

"Here, sir," said Cobweb.

"Good Mr. Cobweb," said the foolish clown, "kill me the red humble-bee on the top of that thistle yonder; and, good Mr. Cobweb, bring me the honey-bag Do not fret yourself too much in the action, Mr. Cobweb, and take care the honey-bag break not; I should be sorry to have you overflown with a honey-bag. Where is Mustard-seed?"

"Here, sir," said Mustard-seed; "what is your will?"

"Nothing," said the clown, "good Mr. Mustard-seed, but to help Mr. Pease-blossom to scratch: I must go to a barber's, Mr. Mustard-seed, for methinks I am marvellous hairy about the face."

"My sweet love," said the queen, "what will you have to eat? I have a venturous fairy shall seek the squirrel's hoard, and fetch you some new nuts."

"I had rather have a handful of dried pease," said the clown, who with his ass's head had got an ass's appetite. "But, I pray, let none of your people disturb me, for I have a mind to sleep."

"Sleep then," said the queen, "and I will wind you in my arms. O how I love you! How I dote upon you!"

When the fairy king saw the clown sleeping in the arms of his queen, he advanced within her sight, and reproached her with having lavished her favours upon an ass.

This she could not deny, as the clown was then sleeping within her arms, with his ass's head crowned by her with flowers.

When Oberon had teased her for some time, he again demanded the changeling boy; which she, ashamed of being discovered by her lord with her new favourite, did not dare to refuse him.

Oberon, having thus obtained the little boy he had so

long wished for to be his page, took pity on the disgraceful situation into which, by his merry contrivance, he had brought his Titania, and threw some of the juice of the other flower into her eyes; and the fairy queen immediately recovered her senses, and wondered at her late dotage, saying how she now loathed the sight of the strange monster.

Oberon likewise took the ass's head from off the clown, and left him to finish his nap with his own fool's head upon his shoulders.

Oberon and his Titania being now perfectly reconciled, he related to her the history of the lovers, and their midnight quarrels; and she agreed to go with him, and see the end of their adventures.

The fairy king and queen found the lovers and their fair ladies, at no great distance from each other, sleeping on a grass-plot; for Puck, to make amends for his former mistake, had contrived with the utmost diligence to bring them all to the same spot, unknown to each other; and he had carefully removed the charm from off the eyes of Lysander with the antidote the fairy king gave to him.

Hermia first awoke, and finding her lost Lysander asleep so near her, was looking at him and wondering at his strange inconstancy. Lysander presently opening his eyes, and seeing his dear Hermia, recovered his reason which the fairy-charm had before clouded, and with his reason, his love for Hermia; and they began to talk over the adventures of the night, doubting if these things had really happened, or if they had both been dreaming the same bewildering dream.

Helena and Demetrius were by this time awake; and a sweet sleep having quieted Helena's disturbed and angry spirits, she listened with delight to the professions of love which Demetrius still made to her, and which, to her surprise as well as pleasure, she began to perceive were sincere.

These fair night-wandering ladies, now no longer rivals, became once more true friends; all the unkind words which had passed were forgiven, and they calmly consulted together what was best to be done in their present situation. It was soon agreed that, as Demetrius had given up his pretensions to Hermia, he should endeavour to prevail upon her father to revoke the cruel sentence of death which had been passed against her. Demetrius was preparing to return to Athens for this friendly purpose, when they were surprised with the sight of Egeus, Hermia's father, who came to the wood in pursuit of his runaway daughter.

When Egeus understood that Demetrius would not now marry his daughter, he no longer opposed her marriage with Lysander, but gave his consent that they should be wedded on the fourth day from that time, being the same day on which Hermia had been condemned to lose her life; and on that same day Helena joyfully agreed to marry her beloved and now faithful Demetrius.

The fairy king and queen, who were invisible spectators of this reconciliation, and now saw the happy ending of the lovers' history brought about through the good offices of Oberon, received so much pleasure, that these kind spirits resolved to celebrate the approaching nuptials with sports and revels throughout their fairy kingdom.

And now, if any are offended with this story of fairies and their pranks, as judging it incredible and strange, they have only to think that they have been asleep and dreaming, and that all these adventures were visions which they saw in their sleep: and I hope none of my readers will be so unreasonable as to be offended with a pretty, harmless Midsummer-Night's Dream.

DRAMATIS PERSONÆ

THESEUS, Duke of Athens.
EGEUS, father to Hermia.
LYSANDER, } in love with Hermia.
DEMETRIUS, }
PHILOSTRATE, master of the revels to Theseus.
QUINCE, a carpenter.
SNUG, a joiner.
BOTTOM, a weaver.
FLUTE, a bellows-mender.
SNOUT, a tinker.
STARVELING, a tailor.

HIPPOLYTA, Queen of the Amazons, betrothed to Theseus.
HERMIA, daughter to Egeus, in love with Lysander.
HELENA, in love with Demetrius.

OBERON, king of the fairies.
TITANIA, queen of the fairies.
PUCK, or Robin Goodfellow.
PEASE-BLOSSOM, }
COBWEB, }
MOTH, } fairies.
MUSTARD-SEED, }

Other fairies attending their King and Queen. Attendants on
Theseus and Hippolyta.

SCENE: *Athens, and a wood near it.*

A MIDSUMMER-NIGHT'S DREAM

ACT I

<small>SCENE I.</small> *Athens. The palace of Theseus*

Enter THESEUS, HIPPOLYTA, PHILOSTRATE, *and*
Attendants

The. Now, fair Hippolyta, our nuptial hour
Draws on apace; four happy days bring in
Another moon: but, O, methinks, how slow
This old moon wanes! she lingers my desires,
Like to a step-dame or a dowager   5
Long withering out a young man's revenue.

Hip. Four days will quickly steep themselves in
night;
Four nights will quickly dream away the time;
And then the moon, like to a silver bow
New-bent in heaven, shall behold the night   10
Of our solemnities.

The.   Go, Philostrate,
Stir up the Athenian youth to merriments;
Awake the pert and nimble spirit of mirth:
Turn melancholy forth to funerals;
The pale companion is not for our pomp.   15

[*Exit Philostrate*

Hippolyta, I woo'd thee with my sword,
And won thy love, doing thee injuries:

21

But I will wed thee in another key,
With pomp, with triumph and with revelling.

Enter EGEUS, HERMIA, LYSANDER, *and* DEMETRIUS

Ege. Happy be Theseus, our renownèd duke!   20
  The. Thanks, good Egeus: what's the news with
      thee?
  Ege. Full of vexation come I, with complaint
Against my child, my daughter Hermia.
Stand forth, Demetrius. My noble lord,
This man hath my consent to marry her.   25
Stand forth, Lysander: and, my gracious duke,
This man hath bewitch'd the bosom of my child:
Thou, thou, Lysander, thou hast given her rhymes
And interchanged love-tokens with my child:
Thou hast by moonlight at her window sung   30
With feigning voice verses of feigning love,
And stolen the impression of her fantasy
With bracelets of thy hair, rings, gawds, conceits,
Knacks, trifles, nosegays, sweetmeats, messengers
Of strong prevailment in unharden'd youth: 35
With cunning hast thou filch'd my daughter's heart,
Turned her obedience, which is due to me,
To stubborn harshness: and, my gracious duke,
Be it so she will not here before your grace
Consent to marry with Demetrius,   40
I beg the ancient privilege of Athens,
As she is mine, I may dispose of her:
Which shall be either to this gentleman
Or to her death, according to our law
Immediately provided in that case.   45
  The. What say you, Hermia? be advised, fair maid:
To you your father should be as a god;
One that composed your beauties, yea, and one
To whom you are but as a form in wax
By him imprinted, and within his power   50

To leave the figure, or disfigure it.
Demetrius is a worthy gentleman.
    Her. So is Lysander.
    The.   In himself he is;
But in this kind, wanting your father's voice,
The other must be held the worthier.   55
    Her. I would my father look'd but with my eyes.
    The. Rather your eyes must with his judgment look.
    Her. I do entreat your grace to pardon me.
I know not by what power I am made bold,
Nor how it may concern my modesty,   60
In such a presence here to plead my thoughts;
But I beseech your grace that I may know
The worst that may befall me in this case,
If I refuse to wed Demetrius.
    The. Either to die the death or to abjure   65
For ever the society of men.
Therefore, fair Hermia, question your desires;
Know of your youth, examine well your blood,
Whether, if you yield not to your father's choice,
You can endure the livery of a nun,   70
For aye to be in shady cloister mew'd,
To live a barren sister all your life,
Chanting faint hymns to the cold fruitless moon.
Thrice-blessed they that master so their blood,
To undergo such maiden pilgrimage;   75
But earthlier happy is the rose distill'd,
Than that which withering on the virgin thorn
Grows, lives and dies in single blessedness.
    Her. So will I grow, so live, so die, my lord,
Ere I will yield my virgin patent up   80
Unto his lordship, whose unwishèd yoke
My soul consents not to give sovereignty.
    The. Take time to pause; and, by the next new
        moon—
The sealing-day betwixt my love and me,

For everlasting bond of fellowship—   85
Upon that day either prepare to die
For disobedience to your father's will,
Or else to wed Demetrius, as he would;
Or on Diana's altar to protest
For aye austerity and single life.   90

Dem. Relent, sweet Hermia: and, Lysander, yield
Thy crazed title to my certain right.

Lys. You have her father's love, Demetrius;
Let me have Hermia's: do you marry him.

Ege. Scornful Lysander! true he hath my love,   95
And what is mine my love shall render him.
And she is mine, and all my right of her
I do estate unto Demetrius.

Lys. I am, my lord, as well derived as he,
As well possess'd; my love is more than his;   100
My fortunes every way as fairly rank'd,
If not with vantage, as Demetrius';
And, which is more than all these boasts can be,
I am beloved of beauteous Hermia:
Why should not I, then, prosecute my right?   105
Demetrius, I 'll avouch it to his head,
Made love to Nedar's daughter, Helena,
And won her soul; and she, sweet lady, dotes,
Devoutly dotes, dotes in idolatry,
Upon this spotted and inconstant man.   110

The. I must confess that I have heard so much,
And with Demetrius thought to have spoke thereof;
But, being over-full of self-affairs,
My mind did lose it.   But, Demetrius, come;
And come, Egeus; you shall go with me,   115
I have some private schooling for you both.
For you, fair Hermia, look you arm yourself
To fit your fancies to your father's will;
Or else the law of Athens yields you up—
Which by no means we may extenuate—   120

To death, or to a vow of single life.
Come, my Hippolyta: what cheer, my love?
Demetrius and Egeus, go along:
I must employ you in some business
Against our nuptial, and confer with you   125
Of something nearly that concerns yourselves.

Ege. With duty and desire we follow you.

> [*Exeunt all but Lysander and Hermia*

Lys. How now, my love! why is your cheek so pale?
How chance the roses there do fade so fast?

Her. Belike for want of rain, which I could well   130
Beteem them from the tempest of my eyes.

Lys. Ay me! for aught that I could ever read,
Could ever hear by tale or history,
The course of true love never did run smooth;
But, either it was different in blood,—   135

Her. O cross! too high to be enthrall'd to low!

Lys. Or else misgraffèd in respect of years,—

Her. O spite! too old to be engaged to young!

Lys. Or else it stood upon the choice of friends,—

Her. O hell! to choose love by another's eyes!   140

Lys. Or, if there were a sympathy in choice,
War, death, or sickness did lay siege to it,
Making it momentany as a sound,
Swift as a shadow, short as any dream;
Brief as the lightning in the collied night,   145
That, in a spleen, unfolds both heaven and earth,
And ere a man hath power to say 'Behold!'
The jaws of darkness do devour it up:
So quick bright things come to confusion.

Her. If then true lovers have been ever cross'd,   150
It stands as an edict in destiny:
Then let us teach our trial patience,
Because it is a customary cross,
As due to love as thoughts, and dreams, and sighs,
Wishes and tears, poor fancy's followers.   155

Lys. A good persuasion: therefore, hear me, Hermia.
I have a widow aunt, a dowager
Of great revénue, and she hath no child:
From Athens is her house remote seven leagues;
And she respects me as her only son.   160
There, gentle Hermia, may I marry thee;
And to that place the sharp Athenian law
Cannot pursue us. If thou lov'st me then,
Steal forth thy father's house to-morrow night;
And in the wood, a league without the town,   165
Where I did meet thee once with Helena,
To do observance to a morn of May,
There will I stay for thee.

    Her.   My good Lysander!
I swear to thee, by Cupid's strongest bow,
By his best arrow with the golden head,   170
By the simplicity of Venus' doves,
By that which knitteth souls and prospers loves,
And by that fire which burn'd the Carthage queen,
When the false Troyan under sail was seen,
By all the vows that ever men have broke,   175
In number more than ever women spoke,
In that same place thou hast appointed me,
To-morrow truly will I meet with thee.

    Lys. Keep promise, love.   Look, here comes Helena.

Enter HELENA

    Her. God speed fair Helena! whither away?   180
    Hel. Call you me fair? that fair again unsay.
Demetrius loves your fair: O happy fair!
Your eyes are lode-stars; and your tongue's sweet
    air
More tuneable than lark to shepherd's ear,
When wheat is green, when hawthorn buds appear. 185
Sickness is catching: O, were favour so,
Yours would I catch, fair Hermia, ere I go;

My ear should catch your voice, my eye your eye,
My tongue should catch your tongue's sweet melody.
Were the world mine, Demetrius being bated,　　190
The rest I 'ld give to be to you translated.
O, teach me how you look, and with what art
You sway the motion of Demetrius' heart.

　　Her. I frown upon him, yet he loves me still.
　　Hel. O that your frowns would teach my smiles
　　　such skill!　　195
　　Her. I give him curses, yet he gives me love.
　　Hel. O that my prayers could such affection move!
　　Her. The more I hate, the more he follows me.
　　Hel. The more I love, the more he hateth me.
　　Her. His folly, Helen, is no fault of mine.　　200
　　Hel. None, but your beauty: would that fault were
　　　mine!

　　Her. Take comfort: he no more shall see my face;
Lysander and myself will fly this place.
Before the time I did Lysander see,
Seem'd Athens as a paradise to me:　　205
O, then, what graces in my love do dwell,
That he hath turn'd a heaven unto a hell!

　　Lys. Helen, to you our minds we will unfold:
To-morrow night, when Phœbe doth behold
Her silver visage in the watery glass,　　210
Decking with liquid pearl the bladed grass,
A time that lovers' flights doth still conceal,
Through Athens' gates have we devised to steal.

　　Her. And in the wood, where often you and I
Upon faint primrose-beds were wont to lie,　　215
Emptying our bosoms of their counsel sweet,
There my Lysander and myself shall meet;
And thence from Athens turn away our eyes,
To seek new friends and stranger companies.
Farewell, sweet playfellow: pray thou for us;　　220
And good luck grant thee thy Demetrius!

Keep word, Lysander: we must starve our sight
From lovers' food till morrow deep midnight.

Lys. I will, my Hermia.   [*Exit Hermia*
                    Helena, adieu:
As you on him, Demetrius dote on you!   [*Exit* 225
    Hel. How happy some o'er other some can be!
Through Athens I am thought as fair as she.
But what of that? Demetrius thinks not so;
He will not know what all but he do know:
And as he errs, doting on Hermia's eyes,   230
So I, admiring of his qualities:
Things base and vile, holding no quantity,
Love can transpose to form and dignity:
Love looks not with the eyes, but with the mind;
And therefore is wing'd Cupid painted blind: 235
Nor hath Love's mind of any judgment taste;
Wings and no eyes figure unheedy haste:
And therefore is Love said to be a child,
Because in choice he is so oft beguiled.
As waggish boys in game themselves forswear,   240
So the boy Love is perjured every where:
For ere Demetrius look'd on Hermia's eyne,
He hail'd down oaths that he was only mine;
And when this hail some heat from Hermia felt,
So he dissolved, and showers of oaths did melt.   245
I will go tell him of fair Hermia's flight:
Then to the wood will he to-morrow night
Pursue her; and for this intelligence
If I have thanks, it is a dear expense:
But herein mean I to enrich my pain,   250
To have his sight thither and back again.   [*Exit*

SCENE 2. *Athens. Quince's house*

Enter QUINCE, SNUG, BOTTOM, FLUTE, SNOUT, *and*
STARVELING

Quin. Is all our company here?

Bot. You were best to call them generally, man by
man, according to the scrip.

Quin. Here is the scroll of every man's name, which
is thought fit, through all Athens, to play in our inter- 5
lude before the duke and the duchess, on his wedding-
day at night.

Bot. First, good Peter Quince, say what the play
treats on, then read the names of the actors; and so
grow to a point.   10

Quin. Marry, our play is, *The most lamentable comedy,
and most cruel death of Pyramus and Thisby.*

Bot. A very good piece of work, I assure you, and
a merry.   Now, good Peter Quince, call forth your
actors by the scroll.   Masters, spread yourselves.   15

Quin. Answer as I call you.   Nick Bottom, the
weaver.

Bot. Ready.   Name what part I am for, and proceed.

Quin. You, Nick Bottom, are set down for Pyramus. 20

Bot. What is Pyramus? a lover, or a tyrant?

Quin. A lover, that kills himself most gallant for
love.

Bot. That will ask some tears in the true performing of it: if I do it, let the audience look to their 25
eyes; I will move storms, I will condole in some
measure.   To the rest: yet my chief humour is for a
tyrant: I could play Ercles rarely, or a part to tear
a cat in, to make all split.

> The raging rocks,   30
> And shivering shocks,

    Shall break the locks
     Of prison gates;
    And Phibbus' car
     Shall shine from far,   35
    And make and mar
     The foolish Fates.

This was lofty! Now name the rest of the players.
This is Ercles' vein, a tyrant's vein; a lover is more
condoling.   40

 Quin. Francis Flute, the bellows-mender.

 Flu. Here, Peter Quince.

 Quin. Flute, you must take Thisby on you.

 Flu. What is Thisby? a wandering knight?

 Quin. It is the lady that Pyramus must love. 45

 Flu. Nay, faith, let not me play a woman; I have
a beard coming.

 Quin. That's all one: you shall play it in a mask,
and you may speak as small as you will.

 Bot. An I may hide my face, let me play Thisby 50
too, I'll speak in a monstrous little voice, 'Thisne,
Thisne'; 'Ah Pyramus, my lover dear! thy Thisby
dear, and lady dear!'

 Quin. No, no; you must play Pyramus: and, Flute,
you Thisby.   55

 Bot. Well, proceed.

 Quin. Robin Starveling, the tailor.

 Star. Here, Peter Quince.

 Quin. Robin Starveling, you must play Thisby's
mother. Tom Snout, the tinker.   60

 Snout. Here, Peter Quince.

 Quin. You, Pyramus' father: myself, Thisby's father.
Snug the joiner; you, the lion's part: and, I hope,
here is a play fitted.

 Snug. Have you the lion's part written? pray you, 65
if it be, give it me, for I am slow of study.

Quin. You may do it extempore, for it is nothing but roaring.

Bot. Let me play the lion too: I will roar, that I will do any man's heart good to hear me; I will roar, 70 that I will make the duke say 'Let him roar again, let him roar again'.

Quin. An you should do it too terribly, you would fright the duchess and the ladies, that they would shriek; and that were enough to hang us all.   75

All. That would hang us, every mother's son.

Bot. I grant you, friends, if that you should fright the ladies out of their wits, they would have no more discretion but to hang us: but I will aggravate my voice so that I will roar you as gently as any suck- 80 ing dove; I will roar you as 't were any nightingale.

Quin. You can play no part but Pyramus: for Pyramus is a sweet-faced man; a proper man, as one shall see in a summer's day; a most lovely gentleman-like man: therefore you must needs play Pyramus.   85

Bot. Well, I will undertake it.   What beard were I best to play it in?

Quin. Why, what you will.

Bot. I will discharge it in either your straw-colour beard, your orange-tawny beard, your purple-in-grain 90 beard, or your French-crown-colour beard, your perfect yellow.

Quin. Some of your French crowns have no hair at all, and then you will play barefaced.   But, masters, here are your parts: and I am to entreat you, request 95 you, and desire you, to con them by to-morrow night; and meet me in the palace wood, a mile without the town, by moonlight; there will we rehearse, for if we meet in the city, we shall be dogged with company, and our devices known.   In the meantime I will draw 100 a bill of properties, such as our play wants.   I pray you, fail me not.

Bot. We will meet; and there we may rehearse most
obscenely and courageously. Take pains; be perfect:
adieu.   105

Quin. At the duke's oak we meet.

Bot. Enough: hold or cut bow-strings.   [*Exeunt*

ACT II

Scene i.   *A wood near Athens*

Enter, from opposite sides, a Fairy, *and* Puck

Puck. How now, spirit! whither wander you?

Fai. Over hill, over dale,
        Thorough bush, thorough brier,
        Over park, over pale,
        Thorough flood, thorough fire,   5
    I do wander every where,
    Swifter than the moonës sphere;
    And I serve the fairy queen,
    To dew her orbs upon the green.
    The cowslips tall her pensioners be: 10
    In their gold coats spots you see;
    Those be rubies, fairy favours,
    In those freckles live their savours:
I must go seek some dewdrops here
And hang a pearl in every cowslip's ear.   15
Farewell, thou lob of spirits; I'll be gone:
Our queen and all her elves come here anon.

Puck. The king doth keep his revels here to-night:
Take heed the queen come not within his sight;
For Oberon is passing fell and wrath,   20
Because that she as her attendant hath
A lovely boy, stolen from an Indian king;
She never had so sweet a changeling;

And jealous Oberon would have the child
Knight of his train, to trace the forests wild;   25
But she perforce withholds the lovèd boy,
Crowns him with flowers, and makes him all her joy:
And now they never meet in grove or green,
By fountain clear, or spangled starlight sheen,
But they do square, that all their elves for fear   30
Creep into acorn-cups, and hide them there.
    Fai. Either I mistake your shape and making quite,
Or else you are that shrewd and knavish sprite
Call'd Robin Goodfellow: are not you he
That frights the maidens of the villagery;   35
Skim milk, and sometimes labour in the quern
And bootless make the breathless housewife churn;
And sometime make the drink to bear no barm;
Mislead night-wanderers, laughing at their harm?
Those that Hobgoblin call you, and sweet Puck,   40
You do their work, and they shall have good luck:
Are not you he?
    Puck.   Thou speak'st aright;
I am that merry wanderer of the night.
I jest to Oberon and make him smile
When I a fat and bean-fed horse beguile,   45
Neighing in likeness of a filly foal:
And sometime lurk I in a gossip's bowl,
In very likeness of a roasted crab,
And when she drinks, against her lips I bob,
And on her withered dewlap pour the ale.   50
The wisest aunt, telling the saddest tale,
Sometime for three-foot stool mistaketh me;
Then slip I from her, and down topples she,
And 'tailor' cries, and falls into a cough;
And then the whole quire hold their hips and laugh,   55
And waxen in their mirth, and neeze, and swear
A merrier hour was never wasted there.
But make room, fairy! here comes Oberon.
    (B 465)   C

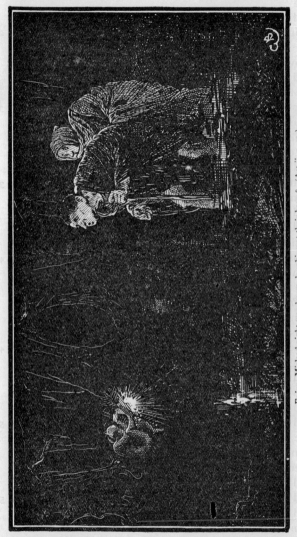

Fairy. Mislead night-wanderers, laughing at their harm?—(Act ii. 1. 39.)

Fai. And here my mistress. Would that he were
gone!

Enter, from one side, OBERON, *with his train; from
the other,* TITANIA, *with hers.*

Obe. Ill met by moonlight, proud Titania. 60
Tita. What, jealous Oberon! Fairies, skip hence:
I have forsworn his bed and company.
Obe. Tarry, rash wanton: am not I thy lord?
Tita. Then I must be thy lady: but I know
When thou hast stolen away from fairy land, 65
And in the shape of Corin sat all day,
Playing on pipes of corn, and versing love
To amorous Phillida. Why art thou here,
Come from the farthest steppe of India?
But that, forsooth, the bouncing Amazon, 70
Your buskin'd mistress and your warrior love,
To Theseus must be wedded, and you come
To give their bed joy and prosperity.
Obe. How canst thou thus, for shame, Titania,
Glance at my credit with Hippolyta, 75
Knowing I know thy love to Theseus?
Didst thou not lead him through the glimmering night,
And make him with fair Ægle break his faith.
With Ariadne and Antiopa?
Tita. These are the forgeries of jealousy: 80
And never, since the middle summer's spring,
Met we on hill, in dale, forest or mead,
By pavèd fountain or by rushy brook,
Or in the beachèd margent of the sea,
To dance our ringlets to the whistling wind, 85
But with thy brawls thou hast disturb'd our sport.
Therefore the winds, piping to us in vain,
As in revenge, have suck'd up from the sea
Contagious fogs; which, falling in the land,
Have every pelting river made so proud, 90

That they have overborne their continents:
The ox hath therefore stretch'd his yoke in vain,
The ploughman lost his sweat, and the green corn
Hath rotted ere his youth attain'd a beard;
The fold stands empty in the drownèd field,   95
And crows are fatted with the murrion flock;
The nine men's morris is fill'd up with mud,
And the quaint mazes in the wanton green,
For lack of tread, are undistinguishable:
The human mortals want their winter here;   100
No night is now with hymn or carol blest:
Therefore the moon, the governess of floods,
Pale in her anger, washes all the air,
That rhéumatic diseases do abound:
And thorough this distemperature we see   105
The seasons alter: hoary-headed frosts
Fall in the fresh lap of the crimson rose,
And on old Hiems' thin and icy crown
An odorous chaplet of sweet summer buds
Is, as in mockery, set: the spring, the summer,   110
The childing autumn, angry winter, change
Their wonted liveries, and the mazèd world,
By their incréase, now knows not which is which:
And this same progeny of evils comes
From our debate, from our dissension;   115
We are their parents and original.
    Obe. Do you amend it then; it lies in you:
Why should Titania cross her Oberon?
I do but beg a little changeling boy,
To be my henchman.
    Tita.   Set your heart at rest: 120
The fairy land buys not the child of me.
His mother was a votaress of my order:
And, in the spicèd Indian air, by night,
Full often hath she gossip'd by my side,
And sat with me on Neptune's yellow sands,   125

Marking the embarked traders on the flood.
But she, being mortal, of that boy did die;
And for her sake do I rear up her boy,
And for her sake I will not part with him.

    Obe. How long within this wood intend you stay? 130
    Tita. Perchance till after Theseus' wedding-day.
If you will patiently dance in our round
And see our moonlight revels, go with us;
If not, shun me, and I will spare your haunts.

    Obe. Give me that boy, and I will go with thee.   135
    Tita. Not for thy fairy kingdom. Fairies, away!
We shall chide downright, if I longer stay.

                  [*Exit Titania with her train*

    Obe. Well, go thy way: thou shalt not from this grove
Till I torment thee for this injury.
My gentle Puck, come hither. Thou remember'st   140
Since once I sat upon a promontory,
And heard a mermaid on a dolphin's back
Uttering such dulcet and harmonious breath
That the rude sea grew civil at her song
And certain stars shot madly from their spheres,   145
To hear the sea-maid's music.

    Puck.   I remember.
    Obe. That very time I saw, but thou couldst not,
Flying between the cold moon and the earth,
Cupid all arm'd: a certain aim he took
At a fair vestal thronèd by the west,   150
And loosed his love-shaft smartly from his bow,
As it should pierce a hundred thousand hearts;
But I might see young Cupid's fiery shaft
Quench'd in the chaste beams of the watery moon,
And the imperial votaress passed on,   155
In maiden meditation, fancy-free.
Yet mark'd I where the bolt of Cupid fell:
It fell upon a little western flower,

Before milk-white, now purple with love's wound,
And maidens call it love-in-idleness.   160
Fetch me that flower; the herb I shew'd thee once:
The juice of it on sleeping eye-lids laid
Will make or man or woman madly dote
Upon the next live creature that it sees.
Fetch me this herb; and be thou here again   165
Ere the leviathan can swim a league.
   Puck. I 'll put a girdle round about the earth
In forty minutes.   [*Exit*
   Obe.   Having once this juice,
I 'll watch Titania when she is asleep,
And drop the liquor of it in her eyes.   170
The next thing then she waking looks upon,
Be it on lion, bear, or wolf, or bull,
On meddling monkey, or on busy ape,
She shall pursue it with the soul of love:
And ere I take this charm from off her sight,   175
As I can take it with another herb,
I 'll make her render up her page to me.
But who comes here? I am invisible;
And I will overhear their conference.

Enter DEMETRIUS, HELENA *following him*

   Dem. I love thee not, therefore pursue me not.   180
Where is Lysander and fair Hermia?
The one I 'll slay, the other slayeth me.
Thou told'st me they were stolen unto this wood;
And here am I, and wood within this wood,
Because I cannot meet my Hermia.   185
Hence, get thee gone, and follow me no more.
   Hel. You draw me, you hard-hearted adamant;
But yet you draw not iron, for my heart
Is true as steel: leave you your power to draw,
And I shall have no power to follow you.   190
   Dem. Do I entice you? do I speak you fair?

Dem. I love thee not, therefore pursue me not.—(Act ii. 1. 180.)

Or, rather, do I not in plainest truth
Tell you, I do not, nor I cannot love you?

   Hel. And even for that do I love you the more.
I am your spaniel; and, Demetrius,   195
The more you beat me, I will fawn on you:
Use me but as your spaniel, spurn me, strike me,
Neglect me, lose me; only give me leave,
Unworthy as I am, to follow you.
What worser place can I beg in your love,—   200
And yet a place of high respect with me,—
Than to be usèd as you use your dog?

   Dem. Tempt not too much the hatred of my spirit,
For I am sick when I do look on thee.

   Hel. And I am sick when I look not on you.   205

   Dem. You do impeach your modesty too much,
To leave the city and commit yourself
Into the hands of one that loves you not.

   Hel. Your virtue is my privilege: for that
It is not night when I do see your face,   210
Therefore I think I am not in the night;
Nor doth this wood lack worlds of company,
For you in my respect are all the world:
Then how can it be said I am alone,
When all the world is here to look on me?   215

   Dem. I 'll run from thee and hide me in the brakes,
And leave thee to the mercy of wild beasts.

   Hel. The wildest hath not such a heart as you.
Run when you will, the story shall be changed:
Apollo flies, and Daphne holds the chase;   220
The dove pursues the griffin; the mild hind
Makes speed to catch the tiger; bootless speed,
When cowardice pursues and valour flies.

   Dem. I will not stay thy questions; let me go:
Or, if thou follow me, do not believe   225
But I shall do thee mischief in the wood.

   Hel. Ay, in the temple, in the town, the field,

You do me mischief. Fie, Demetrius!
Your wrongs do set a scandal on my sex:
We cannot fight for love, as men may do;   230
We should be woo'd and were not made to woo.
                              [*Exit Demetrius*
I 'll follow thee and make a heaven of hell,
To die upon the hand I love so well.   [*Exit*
    Obe. Fare thee well, nymph; ere he do leave this
            grove,
Thou shalt fly him, and he shall seek thy love.   235

                    Re-enter PUCK

Hast thou the flower there? Welcome, wanderer.
    Puck. Ay, there it is.
    Obe.   I pray thee, give it me.
I know a bank whereon the wild thyme blows,
Where oxlips and the nodding violet grows,
Quite over-canopied with lush woodbine,   240
With sweet musk-roses and with eglantine:
There sleeps Titania sometime of the night,
Lull'd in these flowers with dances and delight;
And there the snake throws her enamell'd skin,
Weed wide enough to wrap a fairy in: 245
And with the juice of this I 'll streak her eyes,
And make her full of hateful fantasies.
Take thou some of it, and seek through this grove:
A sweet Athenian lady is in love
With a disdainful youth: anoint his eyes;   250
But do it when the next thing he espies
May be the lady: thou shalt know the man
By the Athenian garments he hath on.
Effect it with some care that he may prove
More fond on her than she upon her love: 255
And look thou meet me ere the first cock crow.
    Puck. Fear not, my lord, your servant shall do so.
                                          [*Exeunt*

SCENE 2. *Another part of the wood*

Enter TITANIA, *with her train*.

Tita. Come, now a roundel and a fairy song;
Then, for the third part of a minute, hence;
Some to kill cankers in the musk-rose buds,
Some war with rere-mice for their leathern wings,
To make my small elves coats, and some keep back 5
The clamorous owl that nightly hoots and wonders
At our quaint spirits. Sing me now asleep;
Then to your offices and let me rest.

SONG

1st Fairy.   You spotted snakes with double tongue,
  Thorny hedgehogs, be not seen;   10
 Newts and blind-worms, do no wrong,
  Come not near our fairy queen.

Chorus.   Philomel, with melody
 Sing in our sweet lullaby;
Lulla, lulla, lullaby, lulla, lulla, lullaby: 15
  Never harm,
  Nor spell nor charm,
 Come our lovely lady nigh;
So, good night, with lullaby.

1st Fairy.   Weaving spiders, come not here;   20
  Hence, you long-legg'd spinners, hence!
 Beetles black, approach not near;
  Worm nor snail, do no offence.

Chorus.   Philomel, with melody, &c.

2nd Fairy. Hence, away! now all is well: 25
 One aloof stand sentinel.
    [*Exeunt Fairies. Titania sleeps.*

Enter OBERON, *and squeezes the flower on Titania's
eyelids*

Obe. What thou seest when thou dost wake,
 Do it for thy true-love sake,

Love and languish for his sake:
Be it ounce, or cat, or bear,   30
Pard, or boar with bristled hair,
In thy eye that shall appear
When thou wak'st, it is thy dear:
Wake when some vile thing is near.   [*Exit*

Enter LYSANDER *and* HERMIA

Lys. Fair love, you faint with wandering in the wood; 35
And to speak troth, I have forgot our way:
We'll rest us, Hermia, if you think it good,
And tarry for the comfort of the day.
Her. Be it so, Lysander: find you out a bed;
For I upon this bank will rest my head.   40
Such separation as may well be said
Becomes a virtuous bachelor and a maid,
So far be distant; and, good night, sweet friend:
Thy love ne'er alter till thy sweet life end!
Lys. Amen, amen, to that fair prayer, say I;   45
And then end life when I end loyalty!
Here is my bed: sleep give thee all his rest!
Her. With half that wish the wisher's eyes be press'd!
[*They sleep*

Enter PUCK

Puck. Through the forest have I gone,
But Athenian found I none,   50
On whose eyes I might approve
This flower's force in stirring love.
Night and silence.—Who is here?
Weeds of Athens he doth wear:
This is he, my master said,   55
Despisèd the Athenian maid;
And here the maiden, sleeping sound,
On the dank and dirty ground.
Pretty soul! she durst not lie
Near this lack-love, this kill-courtesy.   60

Puck. And here the maiden, sleeping sound.—(Act ii. 2. 57.)

> Churl, upon thy eyes I throw
> All the power this charm doth owe.
> When thou wak'st, let love forbid
> Sleep his seat on thy eyelid:
> So awake when I am gone; 65
> For I must now to Oberon. [*Exit*

Enter DEMETRIUS *and* HELENA, *running*

Hel. Stay, though thou kill me, sweet Demetrius.
Dem. I charge thee, hence, and do not haunt me
thus.
Hel. O, wilt thou darkling leave me? do not so.
Dem. Stay, on thy peril: I alone will go. [*Exit* 70
Hel. O, I am out of breath in this fond chase!
The more my prayer, the lesser is my grace.
Happy is Hermia, wheresoe'er she lies;
For she hath blessèd and attractive eyes.
How came her eyes so bright? Not with salt tears: 75
If so, my eyes are oftener wash'd than hers.
No, no, I am as ugly as a bear;
For beasts that meet me run away for fear;
Therefore no marvel though Demetrius
Do, as a monster, fly my presence thus. 80
What wicked and dissembling glass of mine
Made me compare with Hermia's sphery eyne?
But who is here? Lysander! on the ground!
Dead? or asleep? I see no blood, no wound.
Lysander, if you live, good sir, awake. 85
Lys. [*Awaking*] And run through fire I will for thy
sweet sake.
Transparent Helen! Nature here shows art,
That through thy bosom makes me see thy heart.
Where is Demetrius? O, how fit a word
Is that vile name to perish on my sword! 90
Hel. Do not say so, Lysander; say not so.

What though he love your Hermia?   Lord, what
    though?
Yet Hermia still loves you: then be content.
    Lys. Content with Hermia! No; I do repent
The tedious minutes I with her have spent.   95
Not Hermia but Helena I love:
Who will not change a raven for a dove?
The will of man is by his reason swayed;
And reason says you are the worthier maid.
Things growing are not ripe until their season: 100
So I, being young, till now ripe not to reason;
And touching now the point of human skill,
Reason becomes the marshal to my will
And leads me to your eyes, where I o'erlook
Love's stories written in love's richest book.   105
    Hel. Wherefore was I to this keen mockery born?
When at your hands did I deserve this scorn?
Is 't not enough, is 't not enough, young man,
That I did never, no, nor never can,
Deserve a sweet look from Demetrius' eye,   110
But you must flout my insufficiency?
Good troth, you do me wrong, good sooth, you do,
In such disdainful manner me to woo.
But fare you well: perforce I must confess
I thought you lord of more true gentleness.   115
O, that a lady, of one man refused,
Should of another therefore be abused!   [*Exit*
    Lys. She sees not Hermia.   Hermia, sleep thou
    there:
And never mayst thou come Lysander near!
For as a surfeit of the sweetest things   120
The deepest loathing to the stomach brings,
Or as the heresies that men do leave
Are hated most of those they did deceive,
So thou, my surfeit and my heresy,
Of all be hated, but the most of me!   125

And, all my powers, address your love and might
To honour Helen and to be her knight!   [*Exit*
  Her. [*Awaking*] Help me, Lysander, help me! do
    thy best
To pluck this crawling serpent from my breast!
Ay me, for pity! what a dream was here!   130
Lysander, look how I do quake with fear:
Methought a serpent eat my heart away,
And you sat smiling at his cruel prey.
Lysander! what, removed? Lysander! lord!
What, out of hearing? gone? no sound, no word?   135
Alack, where are you? speak, an if you hear;
Speak, of all loves! I swoon almost with fear.
No? then I well perceive you are not nigh:
Either death or you I'll find immediately.   [*Exit*

ACT III

SCENE I. *The wood. Titania lying asleep*

Enter QUINCE, SNUG, BOTTOM, FLUTE, SNOUT, *and*
STARVELING

  Bot. Are we all met?
  Quin. Pat, pat; and here's a marvellous convenient
place for our rehearsal. This green plot shall be our
stage, this hawthorn-brake our tiring-house; and we
will do it in action as we will do it before the duke. 5
  Bot. Peter Quince,—
  Quin. What sayest thou, bully Bottom?
  Bot. There are things in this comedy of Pyramus
and Thisby that will never please. First, Pyramus
must draw a sword to kill himself; which the ladies 10
cannot abide. How answer you that?
  Snout. By'r lakin, a parlous fear.

Star. I believe we must leave the killing out, when all is done.

Bot. Not a whit: I have a device to make all well. 15
Write me a prologue; and let the prologue seem to
say, we will do no harm with our swords, and that
Pyramus is not killed indeed; and, for the more better
assurance, tell them that I Pyramus am not Pyramus,
but Bottom the weaver: this will put them out of fear. 20

Quin. Well, we will have such a prologue; and it
shall be written in eight and six.

Bot. No, make it two more; let it be written in
eight and eight.

Snout. Will not the ladies be afeard of the lion?   25

Star. I fear it, I promise you.

Bot. Masters, you ought to consider with yourselves:
to bring in—God shield us!—a lion among ladies, is
a most dreadful thing; for there is not a more fearful
wild-fowl than your lion living; and we ought to look 30
to 't.

Snout. Therefore another prologue must tell he is
not a lion.

Bot. Nay, you must name his name, and half his
face must be seen through the lion's neck: and he 35
himself must speak through, saying thus, or to the
same defect,—'Ladies',—or 'Fair ladies,—I would
wish you',—or 'I would request you,—or 'I would
entreat you,—not to fear, not to tremble: my life for
yours. If you think I come hither as a lion, it were 40
pity of my life: no, I am no such thing; I am a man
as other men are'; and there, indeed, let him name
his name, and tell them plainly he is Snug the joiner.

Quin. Well, it shall be so. But there is two hard
things; that is, to bring the moonlight into a chamber; 45
for, you know, Pyramus and Thisby meet by moonlight.

Snout. Doth the moon shine that night we play our
play?

Bot. I Pyramus am not Pyramus, but Bottom the weaver.—(Act iii. 1. 19.)

Bot. A calendar, a calendar! look in the almanac; find out moonshine, find out moonshine.   50

Quin. Yes, it doth shine that night.

Bot. Why, then may you leave a casement of the great chamber window, where we play, open, and the moon may shine in at the casement.

Quin. Ay; or else one must come in with a bush 55 of thorns and a lanthorn, and say he comes to disfigure, or to present, the person of Moonshine. Then, there is another thing: we must have a wall in the great chamber; for Pyramus and Thisby, says the story, did talk through the chink of a wall.   60

Snout. You can never bring in a wall. What say you, Bottom?

Bot. Some man or other must present Wall: and let him have some plaster, or some loam, or some rough-cast about him, to signify wall; and let him 65 hold his fingers thus, and through that cranny shall Pyramus and Thisby whisper.

Quin. If that may be, then all is well. Come, sit down, every mother's son, and rehearse your parts. Pyramus, you begin: when you have spoken your 70 speech, enter into that brake: and so every one according to his cue.

Enter PUCK *behind*

Puck. What hempen home-spuns have we swaggering here,

So near the cradle of the fairy queen?

What, a play toward! I'll be an auditor;   75

An actor too perhaps, if I see cause.

Quin. Speak, Pyramus. Thisby, stand forth.

Bot. (*as Pyr.*) Thisby, the flowers of odious savours sweet,--

Quin. Odours, odours.

Pyr.   ——odours savours sweet: 80
    So hath thy breath, my dearest Thisby dear.
  But hark, a voice! stay thou but here awhile,
  And by and by I will to thee appear.   [*Exit.*

Puck. A stranger Pyramus than e'er played here.
                              [*Aside, and exit.*
Flu. Must I speak now?   85
Quin. Ay, marry, must you; for you must understand he goes but to see a noise that he heard, and
is to come again.

Flu. (*as This.*) Most radiant Pyramus, most lily-white of hue,
    Of colour like the red rose on triumphant brier,   90
  Most brisky juvenal and eke most lovely Jew,
    As true as truest horse that yet would never tire,
  I'll meet thee, Pyramus, at Ninny's tomb.

Quin. 'Ninus' tomb', man: why you must not speak
that yet; that you answer to Pyramus: you speak all 95
your part at once, cues and all.   Pyramus enter: your
cue is past; it is, 'never tire'.

This. O,—As true as truest horse, that yet would never tire.

Re-enter PUCK, *and* BOTTOM *with an ass's head*

Pyr. If I were fair, Thisby, I were only thine.

Quin. O monstrous! O strange! we are haunted. 100
Pray, masters! fly, masters! Help!
    [*Exeunt Quince, Snug, Flute, Snout, and Starveling*
Puck. I'll follow you, I'll lead you about a round,
  Through bog, through bush, through brake, through
      brier:
Sometime a horse I'll be, sometime a hound,
  A hog, a headless bear, sometime a fire;   105
And neigh, and bark, and grunt, and roar, and burn,
Like horse, hound, hog, bear, fire, at every turn.
                                            [*Exit*
Bot. Why do they run away? this is a knavery of
them to make me afeard.

Re-enter SNOUT

Snout. O Bottom, thou art changed! what do I see 110
on thee?

Bot. What do you see? you see an ass-head of your
own, do you?   [*Exit Snout*

Re-enter QUINCE

Quin. Bless thee, Bottom! bless thee! thou art
translated.   [*Exit* 115

Bot. I see their knavery: this is to make an ass of
me; to fright me, if they could. But I will not stir
from this place, do what they can: I will walk up and
down here, and I will sing, that they shall hear I am
not afraid.   [*Sings* 120

> The ousel cock so black of hue,
>   With orange-tawny bill,
> The throstle with his note so true,
>   The wren with little quill,—

Tita. [*Awaking*] What angel wakes me from my
    flowery bed?   125
Bot. [*Sings*]

> The finch, the sparrow and the lark,
>   The plain-song cuckoo gray,
> Whose note full many a man doth mark,
>   And dares not answer nay;—

for, indeed, who would set his wit to so foolish a bird? 130
who would give a bird the lie, though he cry 'cuckoo'
never so?

Tita. I pray thee, gentle mortal, sing again:
Mine ear is much enamour'd of thy note;
So is mine eye enthrallèd to thy shape;   135
And thy fair virtue's force perforce doth move me
On the first view to say, to swear, I love thee.

Bot. Methinks, mistress, you should have little reason
for that: and yet, to say the truth, reason and love keep
little company together now-a-days; the more the pity 140

Quin. Bless thee, Bottom! bless thee! thou art translated.—(Act iii. 1. 114, 115.)

that some honest neighbours will not make them friends.
Nay, I can gleek upon occasion.

Tita. Thou art as wise as thou art beautiful.

Bot. Not so, neither: but if I had wit enough to get
out of this wood, I have enough to serve mine own 145
turn.

Tita. Out of this wood do not desire to go:
Thou shalt remain here, whether thou wilt or no.
I am a spirit of no common rate:
The summer still doth tend upon my state;   150
And I do love thee: therefore, go with me;
I 'll give thee fairies to attend on thee,
And they shall fetch thee jewels from the deep,
And sing while thou on pressèd flowers dost sleep:
And I will purge thy mortal grossness so   155
That thou shalt like an airy spirit go.
Pease-blossom! Cobweb! Moth! and Mustard-seed!

Enter PEASE-BLOSSOM, COBWEB, MOTH, *and*
MUSTARD-SEED

Peas. Ready.

Cob.   And I.

Moth.   And I.

Mus.   And I.

All.   Where shall we go?

Tita. Be kind and courteous to this gentleman;
Hop in his walks, and gambol in his eyes;   160
Feed him with apricocks and dewberries,
With purple grapes, green figs, and mulberries;
The honey-bags steal from the humble-bees,
And for night-tapers crop their waxen thighs
And light them at the fiery glow-worm's eyes,   165
To have my love to bed and to arise;
And pluck the wings from painted butterflies
To fan the moonbeams from his sleeping eyes:
Nod to him, elves, and do him courtesies.

Peas. Hail, mortal!   170
Cob. Hail!
Moth. Hail!
Mus. Hail!
Bot. I cry your worships mercy, heartily: I beseech
your worship's name.   175
Cob. Cobweb.
Bot. I shall desire you of more acquaintance, good
Master Cobweb; if I cut my finger, I shall make bold
with you.   Your name, honest gentleman?
Peas. Pease-blossom.   180
Bot.   I pray you, commend me to Mistress Squash,
your mother, and to Master Peascod, your father.   Good
Master Pease - blossom, I shall desire you of more
acquaintance too.   Your name, I beseech you, sir?
Mus. Mustard-seed.   185
Bot. Good Master Mustard-seed, I know your patience
well: that same cowardly, giant-like ox-beef hath
devoured many a gentleman of your house: I promise
you your kindred hath made my eyes water ere now.   I
desire your more acquaintance, good Master Mustard- 190
seed.
Tita. Come, wait upon him; lead him to my bower.
The moon methinks looks with a watery eye;
And when she weeps, weeps every little flower,
Lamenting some enforcèd chastity.   195
Tie up my love's tongue, bring him silently.   [*Exeunt*

SCENE 2.   *Another part of the wood*

Enter OBERON

Obe. I wonder if Titania be awaked;
Then, what it was that next came in her eye,
Which she must dote on in extremity.
Here comes my messenger.

Enter PUCK

                              How now, mad spirit!
What night-rule now about this haunted grove?   5
  Puck. My mistress with a monster is in love.
Near to her close and consecrated bower,
While she was in her dull and sleeping hour,
A crew of patches, rude mechanicals,
That work for bread upon Athenian stalls,   10
Were met together to rehearse a play
Intended for great Theseus' nuptial-day.
The shallowest thick-skin of that barren sort,
Who Pyramus presented in their sport,
Forsook his scene and enter'd in a brake: 15
When I did him at this advantage take,
An ass's nole I fixèd on his head:
Anon his Thisbe must be answerèd,
And forth my mimic comes. When they him spy,
As wild geese that the creeping fowler eye,   20
Or russet-pated choughs, many in sort,
Rising and cawing at the gun's report,
Sever themselves and madly sweep the sky,
So, at his sight, away his fellows fly;
And, at our stamp, here o'er and o'er one falls;   25
He murder cries, and help from Athens calls.
Their sense thus weak, lost with their fears thus
      strong,
Made senseless things begin to do them wrong;
For briers and thorns at their apparel snatch;
Some, sleeves,—some, hats;—from yielders all things
      catch.   30
I led them on in this distracted fear,
And left sweet Pyramus translated there:
When in that moment, so it came to pass,
Titania waked and straightway loved an ass.
  Obe. This falls out better than I could devise.   35

But hast thou yet latch'd the Athenian's eyes
With the love-juice, as I did bid thee do?
   Puck. I took him sleeping,—that is finish'd too,—
And the Athenian woman by his side;
That, when he waked, of force she must be eyed.   40

Enter HERMIA and DEMETRIUS

   Obe. Stand close: this is the same Athenian.
   Puck. This is the woman, but not this the man.
   Dem. O, why rebuke you him that loves you so?
Lay breath so bitter on your bitter foe.
   Her. Now I but chide; but I should use thee worse, 45
For thou, I fear, hast given me cause to curse.
If thou hast slain Lysander in his sleep,
Being o'er shoes in blood, plunge in the deep,
And kill me too.
The sun was not so true unto the day   50
As he to me: would he have stolen away
From sleeping Hermia? I'll believe as soon
This whole earth may be bored; and that the moon
May through the centre creep and so displease
Her brother's noontide with the Antipodes.   55
It cannot be but thou hast murder'd him;
So should a murderer look, so dead, so grim.
   Dem. So should the murder'd look, and so should I,
Pierced through the heart with your stern cruelty:
Yet you, the murderer, look as bright, as clear,   60
As yonder Venus in her glimmering sphere.
   Her. What's this to my Lysander? where is he?
Ah, good Demetrius, wilt thou give him me?
   Dem. I had rather give his carcass to my hounds.
   Her. Out, dog! out, cur! thou driv'st me past the
      bounds   65
Of maiden's patience. Hast thou slain him, then?
Henceforth be never number'd among men!
O, once tell true, tell true, even for my sake!

Her. Out, dog! out, cur! thou driv'st me past the bounds
Of maiden's patience.—(Act iii. 2. 65, 66.)

Durst thou have look'd upon him being awake,
And hast thou kill'd him sleeping? O brave touch! 70
Could not a worm, an adder, do so much?
An adder did it; for with doubler tongue
Than thine, thou serpent, never adder stung.

Dem. You spend your passion on a misprised mood:
I am not guilty of Lysander's blood; 75
Nor is he dead, for aught that I can tell.

Her. I pray thee, tell me, then, that he is well.

Dem. An if I could, what should I get therefor?

Her. A privilege, never to see me more.
And from thy hated presence part I so: 80
See me no more, whether he be dead or no.   [*Exit*

Dem. There is no following her in this fierce vein:
Here therefore for a while I will remain.
So sorrow's heaviness doth heavier grow
For debt that bankrupt sleep doth sorrow owe, 85
Which now in some slight measure it will pay,
If for his tender here I make some stay.
                    [*Lies down and sleeps*

Obe. What hast thou done? thou hast mistaken quite
And laid the love-juice on some true-love's sight:
Of thy misprision must perforce ensue 90
Some true love turn'd, and not a false turn'd true.

Puck. Then fate o'er-rules, that, one man holding troth,
A million fail, confounding oath on oath.

Obe. About the wood go swifter than the wind,
And Helena of Athens look thou find: 95
All fancy-sick she is, and pale of cheer,
With sighs of love, that costs the fresh blood dear:
By some illusion see thou bring her here:
I'll charm her eyes against she do appear.

Puck. I go, I go; look how I go, 100
Swifter than arrow from the Tartar's bow.   [*Exit*

Obe. Flower of this purple dye,
　　Hit with Cupid's archery,

　　　　　　[*Squeezes the flower-juice on
　　　　　　　　Demetrius' eyelids*

　　Sink in apple of his eye.
　　When his love he doth espy,　　　　　105
　　Let her shine as gloriously
　　As the Venus of the sky.
　　When thou wakest, if she be by,
　　Beg of her for remedy.

Re-enter PUCK

Puck. Captain of our fairy band,　　　　110
　　Helena is here at hand;
　　And the youth, mistook by me,
　　Pleading for a lover's fee.
　　Shall we their fond pageant see?
　　Lord, what fools these mortals be!　　115
Obe. Stand aside: the noise they make
　　Will cause Demetrius to awake.
Puck. Then will two at once woo one;
　　That must needs be sport alone;
　　And those things do best please me　　120
　　That befall preposterously.

Enter LYSANDER *and* HELENA

Lys. Why should you think that I should woo in
　　scorn?
Scorn and derision never come in tears:
Look, when I vow, I weep; and vows so born,
　　In their nativity all truth appears.　　125
How can these things in me seem scorn to you,
Bearing the badge of faith, to prove them true?
　Hel. You do advance your cunning more and more.
　　When truth kills truth. O devilish-holy fray!

These vows are Hermia's: will you give her o'er?   130
  Weigh oath with oath, and you will nothing weigh:
Your vows to her and me, put in two scales,
Will even weigh, and both as light as tales.
  Lys. I had no judgment when to her I swore.
  Hel. Nor none, in my mind, now you give her
    o'er.   135
  Lys. Demetrius loves her, and he loves not you.
  Dem. [*Awaking*] O Helen, goddess, nymph, perféct,
    divine!
To what, my love, shall I compare thine eyne?
Crystal is muddy. O, how ripe in show
Thy lips, those kissing cherries, tempting grow!   140
That pure congealed white, high Taurus' snow,
Fann'd with the eastern wind, turns to a crow
When thou hold'st up thy hand: O, let me kiss
This princess of pure white, this seal of bliss!
  Hel. O spite! O hell! I see you all are bent   145
To set against me for your merriment:
If you were civil, and knew courtesy,
You would not do me thus much injury.
Can you not hate me, as I know you do,
But you must join in souls to mock me too?   150
If you were men, as men you are in show,
You would not use a gentle lady so;
To vow, and swear, and superpraise my parts,
When I am sure you hate me with your hearts.
You both are rivals, and love Hermia;   155
And now both rivals, to mock Helena:
A trim exploit, a manly enterprise,
To conjure tears up in a poor maid's eyes
With your derision! none of noble sort
Would so offend a virgin, and extort   160
A poor soul's patience, all to make you sport.
  Lys. You are unkind, Demetrius; be not so;
For you love Hermia; this you know I know:

And here, with all good will, with all my heart,
In Hermia's love I yield you up my part;   165
And yours of Helena to me bequeath,
Whom I do love, and will do till my death.

    Hel. Never did mockers waste more idle breath.

    Dem. Lysander, keep thy Hermia; I will none:
If e'er I loved her, all that love is gone.   170
My heart to her but as guest-wise sojourn'd,
And now to Helen is it home return'd,
There to remain.

    Lys.   Helen, it is not so.

    Dem. Disparage not the faith thou dost not know,
Lest, to thy peril, thou aby it dear.   175
Look, where thy love comes; yonder is thy dear.

Re-enter HERMIA

    Her. Dark night, that from the eye his function
      takes,
The ear more quick of apprehension makes;
Wherein it doth impair the seeing sense,
It pays the hearing double recompense.   180
Thou art not by mine eye, Lysander, found;
Mine ear, I thank it, brought me to thy sound.
But why unkindly didst thou leave me so?

    Lys. Why should he stay, whom love doth press
      to go?

    Her. What love could press Lysander from my side? 185

    Lys. Lysander's love, that would not let him bide,
Fair Helena, who more engilds the night
Than all yon fiery oes and eyes of light.
Why seek'st thou me? could not this make thee know,
The hate I bear thee made me leave thee so?   190

    Her. You speak not as you think: it cannot be.

    Hel. Lo, she is one of this confederacy!
Now I perceive they have conjoin'd all three
To fashion this false sport. in spite of me.

Injurious Hermia! most ungrateful maid!   195
Have you conspired, have you with these contrived
To bait me with this foul derision?
Is all the counsel that we two have shared,
The sisters' vows, the hours that we have spent,
When we have chid the hasty-footed time   200
For parting us,—O, and is all forgot?
All school-days' friendship, childhood innocence?
We, Hermia, like two artificial gods,
Have with our neelds created both one flower,
Both on one sampler, sitting on one cushion,   205
Both warbling of one song, both in one key,
As if our hands, our sides, voices and minds,
Had been incorporate. So we grew together,
Like to a double cherry, seeming parted,
But yet an union in partition;   210
Two lovely berries moulded on one stem:
So, with two seeming bodies, but one heart;
Two of the first, like coats in heraldry,
Due but to one, and crownèd with one crest.
And will you rent our ancient love asunder,   215
To join with men in scorning your poor friend?
It is not friendly, 't is not maidenly:
Our sex, as well as I, may chide you for it,
Though I alone do feel the injury.
     Her. I am amazèd at your passionate words.   220
I scorn you not: it seems that you scorn me.
     Hel. Have you not set Lysander, as in scorn,
To follow me and praise my eyes and face?
And made your other love, Demetrius,
Who e'en but now did spurn me with his foot,   225
To call me goddess, nymph, divine and rare,
Precious, celestial? Wherefore speaks he this
To her he hates? and wherefore doth Lysander
Deny your love, so rich within his soul,
And tender me, forsooth, affection,   230

Hel.   O, and is all forgot?
All school-days' friendship, childhood innocence?
                   —(Act iii. 2. 201, 202.)

But by your setting on, by your consent?
What though I be not so in grace as you,
So hung upon with love, so fortunate,
But miserable most, to love unloved?
This you should pity rather than despise.   235

Her. I understand not what you mean by this.

Hel. Ay, do, perséver, counterfeit sad looks,
Make mouths upon me when I turn my back;
Wink each at other; hold the sweet jest up:
This sport, well carried, shall be chronicled.   240
If you have any pity, grace, or manners,
You would not make me such an argument.
But fare ye well: 'tis partly my own fault;
Which death or absence soon shall remedy.

Lys. Stay, gentle Helena; hear my excuse: 245
My love, my life, my soul, fair Helena!

Hel. O excellent!

Her.   Sweet, do not scorn her so.

Dem. If she cannot entreat, I can compel.

Lys. Thou canst compel no more than she entreat:
Thy threats have no more strength than her weak
     prayers.   250
Helen, I love thee; by my life, I do:
I swear by that which I will lose for thee,
To prove him false that says I love thee not.

Dem. I say I love thee more than he can do.

Lys. If thou say so, withdraw, and prove it too.   255

Dem. Quick, come!

Her.   Lysander, whereto tends all this?

Lys. Away, you Ethiope!

Dem.   No, no; he'll——sir,
Seem to break loose; take on as you would follow,
But yet come not: you are a tame man, go!

Lys. Hang off, thou cat, thou burr! vile thing, let
     loose,   260
Or I will shake thee from me like a serpent!

Her. Why are you grown so rude? what change is
  this?
Sweet love,—
  Lys.   Thy love! out, tawny Tartar, out!
Out, loathèd medicine! hated potion, hence!
  Her. Do you not jest?
  Hel.   Yes, sooth; and so do you. 265
  Lys. Demetrius, I will keep my word with thee.
  Dem. I would I had your bond, for I perceive
A weak bond holds you: I'll not trust your word.
  Lys. What, should I hurt her, strike her, kill her
  dead?
Although I hate her, I'll not harm her so.   270
  Her. What, can you do me greater harm than hate?
Hate me! wherefóre? O me! what news, my love?
Am not I Hermia? are not you Lysander?
I am as fair now as I was erewhile.
Since night you loved me; yet since night you left me: 275
Why, then you left me—O, the gods forbid!—
In earnest, shall I say?
  Lys.   Ay, by my life;
And never did desire to see thee more.
Therefore be out of hope, of question, doubt:
Be certain, nothing truer: 'tis no jest   280
That I do hate thee, and love Helena.
  Her. O me! you juggler! you canker-blossom!
You thief of love! what, have you come by night
And stolen my love's heart from him?
  Hel.   Fine, i' faith!
Have you no modesty, no maiden shame,   285
No touch of bashfulness? What, will you tear
Impatient answers from my gentle tongue?
Fie, fie! you counterfeit, you puppet, you!
  Her. Puppet? why so? ay, that way goes the game.
Now I perceive that she hath made compare   290
Between our statures; she hath urged her height;

And with her personage, her tall personage,
Her height, forsooth, she hath prevail'd with him.
And are you grown so high in his esteem,
Because I am so dwarfish and so low?   295
How low am I, thou painted maypole? speak;
How low am I? I am not yet so low
But that my nails can reach unto thine eyes.

Hel. I pray you, though you mock me, gentlemen,
Let her not hurt me: I was never curst;   300
I have no gift at all in shrewishness;
I am a right maid for my cowardice:
Let her not strike me. You perhaps may think,
Because she is something lower than myself,
That I can match her.

Her.   Lower! hark, again.   305

Hel. Good Hermia, do not be so bitter with me.
I evermore did love you, Hermia,
Did ever keep your counsels, never wrong'd you;
Save that, in love unto Demetrius,
I told him of your stealth unto this wood.   310
He follow'd you; for love I follow'd him;
But he hath chid me hence, and threaten'd me
To strike me, spurn me, nay, to kill me too:
And now, so you will let me quiet go,
To Athens will I bear my folly back   315
And follow you no further: let me go:
You see how simple and how fond I am.

Her. Why, get you gone: who is 't that hinders
    you?

Hel. A foolish heart, that I leave here behind.

Her. What, with Lysander?

Hel.   With Demetrius.   320

Lys. Be not afraid; she shall not harm thee, Helena.

Dem. No, sir, she shall not, though you take her
    part.

Hel. O, when she 's angry, she is keen and shrewd!

She was a vixen when she went to school;
And though she be but little, she is fierce.   325

Her. 'Little' again! nothing but 'low' and 'little'!
Why will you suffer her to flout me thus?
Let me come to her.

Lys.   Get you gone, you dwarf;
You minimus, of hindering knot-grass made;
You bead, you acorn.

Dem.   You are too officious   330
In her behalf that scorns your services.
Let her alone: speak not of Helena;
Take not her part; for, if thou dost intend
Never so little show of love to her,
Thou shalt aby it.

Lys.   Now she holds me not;   335
Now follow, if thou darest, to try whose right,
Of thine or mine, is most in Helena.

Dem. Follow! nay, I'll go with thee, cheek by jole.
                    [*Exeunt Lysander and Demetrius*

Her. You, mistress, all this coil is 'long of you:
Nay, go not back.

Hel.   I will not trust you, I,   340
Nor longer stay in your curst company.
Your hands than mine are quicker for a fray,
My legs are longer though, to run away.   [*Exit*

Her. I am amaz'd, and know not what to say.
                    [*Exit*

Obe. This is thy negligence: still thou mistak'st,   345
Or else committ'st thy knaveries wilfully.

Puck. Believe me, king of shadows, I mistook.
Did not you tell me I should know the man
By the Athenian garments he had on?
And so far blameless proves my enterprise,   350
That I have 'nointed an Athenian's eyes;
And so far am I glad it so did sort
As this their jangling I esteem a sport.

Obe. Thou see'st these lovers seek a place to fight:
Hie therefore, Robin, overcast the night;   355
The starry welkin cover thou anon
With drooping fog as black as Acheron,
And lead these testy rivals so astray
As one come not within another's way.
Like to Lysander sometime frame thy tongue,   360
Then stir Demetrius up with bitter wrong;
And sometime rail thou like Demetrius;
And from each other look thou lead them thus,
Till o'er their brows death-counterfeiting sleep
With leaden legs and batty wings doth creep: 365
Then crush this herb into Lysander's eye;
Whose liquor hath this virtuous property,
To take from thence all error with his might,
And make his eyeballs roll with wonted sight.
When they next wake, all this derision   370
Shall seem a dream and fruitless vision,
And back to Athens shall the lovers wend,
With league whose date till death shall never end.
Whiles I in this affair do thee employ,
I 'll to my queen and beg her Indian boy;   375
And then I will her charmed eye release
From monster's view, and all things shall be peace.
Puck. My fairy lord, this must be done with haste,
For night's swift dragons cut the clouds full fast,
And yonder shines Aurora's harbinger;   380
At whose approach, ghosts, wandering here and there,
Troop home to churchyards: damnèd spirits all,
That in crossways and floods have burial,
Already to their wormy beds are gone;
For fear lest day should look their shames upon,   385
They wilfully themselves exile from light,
And must for aye consort with black-brow'd night.
Obe. But we are spirits of another sort:
I with the morning's love have oft made sport,

And, like a forester, the groves may tread,   390
Even till the eastern gate, all fiery-red,
Opening on Neptune with fair blessèd beams,
Turns into yellow gold his salt green streams.
But, notwithstanding, haste; make no delay:
We may effect this business yet ere day.   [*Exit* 395

   Puck.   Up and down, up and down,
            I will lead them up and down:
            I am fear'd in field and town:
            Goblin, lead them up and down.
Here comes one.   400

Re-enter LYSANDER

Lys. Where art thou, proud Demetrius? speak thou
   now.
Puck. Here, villain; drawn and ready. Where art
   thou?
Lys. I will be with thee straight.
Puck.   Follow me, then,
To plainer ground.
              [*Exit Lysander, as following the voice*

Re-enter DEMETRIUS

Dem.   Lysander! speak again:
Thou runaway, thou coward, art thou fled?   405
Speak! In some bush? Where dost thou hide thy
   head?
Puck. Thou coward, art thou bragging to the stars,
Telling the bushes that thou look'st for wars,
And wilt not come? Come, recreant; come, thou
   child;
I 'll whip thee with a rod: he is defiled   410
That draws a sword on thee.
Dem.   Yea, art thou there?
Puck. Follow my voice: we 'll try no manhood here.
              [*Exeunt*

Dem.   Lysander! speak again:
Thou runaway, thou coward, art thou fled?—(Act iii. 2. 404, 405.)

Re-enter LYSANDER

Lys. He goes before me and still dares me on:
When I come where he calls, then he is gone.
The villain is much lighter-heel'd than I: 415
I follow'd fast, but faster he did fly;
That fallen am I in dark uneven way,
And here will rest me. [*Lies down.*] Come, thou
    gentle day!
For if but once thou show me thy grey light,
I'll find Demetrius and revenge this spite.   [*Sleeps* 420

Re-enter PUCK *and* DEMETRIUS

Puck. Ho, ho, ho, ho! Coward, why com'st thou
    not?
Dem. Abide me, if thou dar'st; for well I wot
Thou runn'st before me, shifting every place,
And dar'st not stand, nor look me in the face.
Where art thou now?
Puck.   Come hither: I am here.   425
Dem. Nay, then, thou mock'st me. Thou shalt buy
    this dear,
If ever I thy face by daylight see:
Now, go thy way. Faintness constraineth me
To measure out my length on this cold bed.
By day's approach look to be visited.   430
              [*Lies down and sleeps*

Re-enter HELENA

Hel. O weary night, O long and tedious night,
    Abate thy hours! Shine comforts from the east,
That I may back to Athens by daylight,
    From these that my poor company detest:
And sleep, that sometimes shuts up sorrow's eye,   435
Steal me awhile from mine own company.
              [*Lies down and sleeps*

Her. Never so weary, never so in woe. —(Act iii. 2. 442.)

73

Puck.   Yet but three? Come one more;
              Tw? of both kinds makes up four.
              Here she comes, curst and sad:
              Cupid is a knavish lad,   440
              Thus to make poor females mad.

                    Re-enter HERMIA

Her. Never so weary, never so in woe,
  Bedabbled with the dew, and torn with briers,
I can no further crawl, no further go;
  My legs can keep no pace with my desires.   445
Here will I rest me till the break of day.
Heavens shield Lysander, if they mean a fray.
                              [*Lies down and sleeps*
Puck.   On the ground
                    Sleep sound:
                    I 'll apply   450
                    To your eye,
                Gentle lover, remedy.
                    [*Squeezing the juice on Lysander's eyes*
                    When thou wakest,
                    Thou takest
                    True delight   455
                    In the sight
              Of thy former lady's eye:
              And the country proverb known,
              That every man should take his own,
              In your waking shall be shown: 460
                    Jack shall have Jill;
                    Nought shall go ill;
The man shall have his mare again, and all shall be
    well.   [*Exit*

ACT IV

Scene i. *The same.* Lysander, Demetrius, Helena,
              and Hermia *lying asleep*

Enter Titania *and* Bottom; Pease-blossom, Cobweb,
    Moth, Mustard-seed, *and other fairies attending;*
    Oberon *behind unseen.*

Tita. Come, sit thee down upon this flowery bed,
    While I thy amiable cheeks do coy,
And stick musk-roses in thy sleek smooth head,
    And kiss thy fair large ears, my gentle joy. ·
  Bot. Where's Pease-blossom?   5
  Peas. Ready.
  Bot. Scratch my head, Pease - blossom. Where's
Mounsier Cobweb?
  Cob. Ready.
  Bot. Mounsier Cobweb, good mounsier, get you 10
your weapons in your hand, and kill me a red-hipped
humble-bee on the top of a thistle; and, good moun-
sier, bring me the honey-bag. Do not fret yourself
too much in the action, mounsier; and, good moun-
sier, have a care the honey-bag break not; I would 15
be loth to have you overflown with a honey - bag,
signior. Where's Mounsier Mustard-seed?
  Mus. Ready.
  Bot. Give me your neaf, Mounsier Mustard - seed.
Pray you, leave your courtesy, good mounsier.   20
  Mus. What's your will?
  Bot. Nothing, good mounsier, but to help Cavalery
Cobweb to scratch. I must to the barber's, mounsier; for methinks I am marvellous hairy about the
face; and I am such a tender ass, if my hair do but 25
tickle me, I must scratch.
  Tita. What, wilt thou hear some music, my sweet
    love?

Bot. I have a reasonable good ear in music.
Let's have the tongs and the bones.   [*Rough music*

Tita. Or say, sweet love, what thou desir'st to eat. 30

Bot. Truly, a peck of provender: I could munch
your good dry oats.   Methinks I have a great desire
to a bottle of hay: good hay, sweet hay, hath no
fellow.

Tita. I have a venturous fairy that shall seek   35
The squirrel's hoard, and fetch thee thence new nuts.

Bot. I had rather have a handful or two of dried
peas.   But, I pray you, let none of your people stir
me: I have an exposition of sleep come upon me.

Tita. Sleep thou, and I will wind thee in my arms. 40
Fairies, be gone, and be all ways away.

[*Exeunt fairies*

So doth the woodbine the sweet honeysuckle
Gently entwist; the female ivy so
Enrings the barky fingers of the elm.
O, how I love thee! how I dote on thee!   45

[*They sleep*

Enter PUCK

Obe. [*Advancing*] Welcome, good Robin.   See'st
    thou this sweet sight?
Her dotage now I do begin to pity:
For, meeting her of late behind the wood,
Seeking sweet favours for this hateful fool,
I did upbraid her, and fall out with her;   50
For she his hairy temples then had rounded
With coronet of fresh and fragrant flowers;
And that same dew, which sometime on the buds
Was wont to swell like round and orient pearls,
Stood now within the pretty flowerets' eyes   55
Like tears, that did their own disgrace bewail.
When I had at my pleasure taunted her
And she in mild terms begg'd my patience,

I then did ask of her her changeling child;
Which straight she gave me, and her fairy sent   60
To bear him to my bower in fairy land.
And now I have the boy, I will undo
This hateful imperfection of her eyes:
And, gentle Puck, take this transformèd scalp
From off the head of this Athenian swain: 65
That he awaking when the other do,
May all to Athens back again repair
And think no more of this night's accidents,
But as the fierce vexation of a dream.
But first I will release the fairy queen.   70

       Be as thou wast wont to be;
                [*Touching her eyes with an herb.*
       See as thou wast wont to see:
       Dian's bud o'er Cupid's flower
       Hath such force and blessèd power.

Now, my Titania; wake you, my sweet queen.   75
   Tita. My Oberon! what visions have I seen!
Methought I was enamour'd of an ass.
   Obe. There lies your love.
   Tita.   How came these things to pass?
O, how mine eyes do loathe his visage now!
   Obe. Silence awhile. Robin, take off this head.   80
Titania, music call; and strike more dead
Than common sleep of all these five the sense.
   Tita. Music, ho! music, such as charmeth sleep!
   Puck. Now, when thou wak'st, with thine own fool's
   eyes peep.   [*Puck takes off the ass's head from
                            Bottom
   Obe. Sound, music! [*Soft music*] Come, my queen,
   take hands with me,   85
And rock the ground whereon these sleepers be.
Now thou and I are new in amity,
And will to-morrow midnight solemnly
Dance in Duke Theseus' house triumphantly,

And bless it to all fair prosperity: 90
There shall the pairs of faithful lovers be
Wedded, with Theseus, all in jollity.
   Puck. Fairy king, attend and mark:
I do hear the morning lark.
   Obe. Then, my queen, in silence sad,   95
Trip we after nightës shade:
We the globe can compass soon,
Swifter than the wandering moon.
   Tita. Come, my lord; and in our flight
Tell me how it came this night,   100
That I sleeping here was found,
With these mortals, on the ground.   [*Exeunt*
                              [*Horns winded within*

Enter THESEUS, HIPPOLYTA, EGEUS, *and train*

   The. Go, one of you, find out the forester;
For now our observation is perform'd;
And since we have the vaward of the day,   105
My love shall hear the music of my hounds.
Uncouple in the valley; let them go:
Dispatch, I say, and find the forester.
                           [*Exit an Attendant*
We will, fair queen, up to the mountain's top,
And mark the musical confusion   110
Of hounds and echo in conjunction.
   Hip. I was with Hercules and Cadmus once,
When in a wood of Crete they bay'd the bear
With hounds of Sparta: never did I hear
Such gallant chiding; for, besides the groves,   115
The skies, the mountains, every region near
Seem'd all one mutual cry: I never heard
So musical a discord, such sweet thunder.
   The. My hounds are bred out of the Spartan kind,
So flew'd, so sanded, and their heads are hung   120

With ears that sweep away the morning dew;
Crook-knee'd, and dew-lapp'd like Thessalian bulls;
Slow in pursuit, but match'd in mouth like bells,
Each under each. A cry more tuneable
Was never holla'd to, nor cheer'd with horn,   125
In Crete, in Sparta, nor in Thessaly:
Judge when you hear.   But, soft! what nymphs are
    these?

Ege. My lord, this is my daughter here asleep;
And this, Lysander; this Demetrius is;
This Helena, old Nedar's Helena: 130
I wonder of their being here together.

The. No doubt they rose up early to observe
The rite of May, and, hea.ing our intent,
Came here in grace of our solemnity.
But speak, Egeus; is not this the day   135
That Hermia should give answer of her choice?

Ege. It is, my lord.

The. Go, bid the huntsmen wake them with their
    horns.

        [*Horns and shout within. Lysander, Demetrius,*
                Helena, and Hermia wake and start up
Good morrow, friends. Saint Valentine is past:
Begin these wood-birds but to couple now?   140

Lys. Pardon, my lord.   [*He and the rest kneel*

The.   I pray you all, stand up.
I know you two are rival enemies:
How comes this gentle concord in the world,
That hatred is so far from jealousy,
To sleep by hate, and fear no enmity?   145

Lys. My lord, I shall reply amazedly,
Half sleep, half waking: but as yet, I swear,
I cannot truly say how I came here;
But, as I think,—for truly would I speak,
And now I do bethink me, so it is,—   150
I came with Hermia hither: our intent

Was to be gone from Athens, where we might,
Without the peril of the Athenian law—

   Ege. Enough, enough, my lord; you have enough:
I beg the law, the law, upon his head.   155
They would have stolen away; they would, Demetrius,
Thereby to have defeated you and me,
You of your wife, and me of my consent,
Of my consent that she should be your wife.

   Dem. My lord, fair Helen told me of their stealth, 160
Of this their purpose hither to this wood;
And I in fury hither follow'd them,
Fair Helena in fancy following me.
But, my good lord, I wot not by what power,—
But by some power it is,—my love to Hermia, 165
Melted as melts the snow, seems to me now
As the remembrance of an idle gawd,
Which in my childhood I did dote upon;
And all the faith, the virtue of my heart,
The object and the pleasure of mine eye, 170
Is only Helena. To her, my lord,
Was I betroth'd ere I saw Hermia:
But, like in sickness, did I loathe this food;
But, as in health, come to my natural taste,
Now I do wish it, love it, long for it, 175
And will for evermore be true to it.

   The. Fair lovers, you are fortunately met:
Of this discourse we more will hear anon.
Egeus, I will overbear your will;
For in the temple, by and by, with us 180
These couples shall eternally be knit:
And, for the morning now is something worn,
Our purposed hunting shall be set aside.
Away with us to Athens; three and three,
We'll hold a feast in great solemnity. 185
Come, Hippolyta.

      [Exeunt Theseus, Hippolyta, Egeus, and train

Dem. These things seem small and undistinguishable,
Like far-off mountains turnèd into clouds.

Her. Methinks I see these things with parted eye,
When every thing seems double.

Hel.　　　　　　　　　　So methinks:　190
And I have found Demetrius like a jewel,
Mine own, and not mine own.

Dem.　　　　　　　　But are you sure
That we are well awake? It seems to me
That yet we sleep, we dream. Do not you think
The duke was here, and bid us follow him?　195

Her. Yea; and my father.

Hel.　　　　　　　　And Hippolyta.

Lys. And he did bid us follow to the temple.

Dem. Why, then, we are awake: let's follow him;
And by the way let us recount our dreams. [*Exeunt*

Bot. [*Awaking*] When my cue comes, call me, and I 200
will answer: my next is, 'Most fair Pyramus'. Heigh-
ho! Peter Quince! Flute, the bellows-mender! Snout,
the tinker! Starveling! God's my life, stolen hence,
and left me asleep! I have had a most rare vision. I
have had a dream, past the wit of man to say what 205
dream it was: man is but an ass, if he go about to ex-
pound this dream. Methought I was—there is no man
can tell what. Methought I was,—and methought I
had,—but man is but a patched fool, if he will offer to
say what methought I had. The eye of man hath not 210
heard, the ear of man hath not seen, man's hand is not
able to taste, his tongue to conceive, nor his heart to
report, what my dream was. I will get Peter Quince to
write a ballad of this dream: it shall be called Bottom's
Dream, because it hath no bottom; and I will sing it 215
in the latter end of the play, before the duke: peradven-
ture, to make it the more gracious, I shall sing it at her
death. [*Exit*

Scene 2. *Athens. A room in Quince's house*

Enter Quince, Flute, Snout, *and* Starveling

Quin. Have you sent to Bottom's house? is he come home yet?

Star. He cannot be heard of. Out of doubt he is transported.

Flu. If he come not, then the play is marred: it goes not forward, doth it?

Quin. It is not possible: you have not a man in all Athens able to discharge Pyramus but he.

Flu. No, he hath simply the best wit of any handi-craft man in Athens.   10

Quin. Yea, and the best person too; and he is a very paragon for a sweet voice.

Enter Snug

Snug. Masters, the duke is coming from the temple, and there is two or three lords and ladies more married: if our sport had gone forward, we had all been made 15 men.

Flu. O sweet bully Bottom! Thus hath he lost six-pence a day during his life; he could not have 'scaped sixpence a day: an the duke had not given him six-pence a day for playing Pyramus, I 'll be hanged; he 20 would have deserved it: sixpence a day in Pyramus, or nothing.

Enter Bottom

Bot. Where are these lads? where are these hearts?

Quin. Bottom! O most courageous day! O most happy hour!   25

Bot. Masters, I am to discourse wonders: but ask me not what; for if I tell you, I am no true Athenian. I will tell you every thing, right as it fell out.

Quin. Let us hear, sweet Bottom.

Bot. Not a word of me. All that I will tell you is, 30

that the duke hath dined.   Get your apparel together,
good strings to your beards, new ribbons to your
pumps; meet presently at the palace; every man look
o'er his part; for the short and the long is, our play

Bot. Masters, I am to discourse wonders: but ask me not what.
—(Act iv. 2. 26, 27.)

is preferred.   In any case, let Thisby have clean linen; 35
and let not him that plays the lion pare his nails, for
they shall hang out for the lion's claws.   And, most
dear actors, eat no onions nor garlic, for we are to
utter sweet breath; and I do not doubt but to hear
them say, it is a sweet comedy.   No more words: 40
away! go, away!   [*Exeunt*

ACT V

Scene i.   *Athens.   The palace of Theseus*

Enter Theseus, Hippolyta, Philostrate, Lords, *and*
Attendants

Hip. 'T is strange, my Theseus, that these lovers
  speak of.

The. More strange than true: I never may believe
These antique fables, nor these fairy toys.
Lovers and madmen have such seething brains,
Such shaping fantasies, that apprehend   5
More than cool reason ever comprehends.
The lunatic, the lover and the poet
Are of imagination all compact:
One sees more devils than vast hell can hold,
That is, the madman: the lover, all as frantic, 10
Sees Helen's beauty in a brow of Egypt:
The poet's eye, in a fine frenzy rolling,
Doth glance from heaven to earth, from earth to
  heaven;
And as imagination bodies forth
The forms of things unknown, the poet's pen   15
Turns them to shapes and gives to airy nothing
A local habitation and a name.
Such tricks hath strong imagination,
That, if it would but apprehend some joy,
It comprehends some bringer of that joy;   20
Or in the night, imagining some fear,
How easy is a bush supposed a bear!

Hip. But all the story of the night told over,
And all their minds transfigured so together,
More witnesseth than fancy's images   25
And grows to something of great constancy;
But, howsoever, strange and admirable.

The. Here come the lovers, full of joy and mirth.

Enter LYSANDER, DEMETRIUS, HERMIA, *and* HELENA

Joy, gentle friends! joy and fresh days of love
Accompany your hearts!
   Lys.   More than to us   30
Wait in your royal walks, your board, your bed!
   The. Come now; what masques, what dances shall
     we have,
To wear away this long age of three hours
Between our after-supper and bed-time?
Where is our usual manager of mirth?   35
What revels are in hand?   Is there no play,
To ease the anguish of a torturing hour?
Call Philostrate.
   Phil.   Here, mighty Theseus.
   The. Say, what abridgement have you for this even-
     ing?
What masque? what music?   How shall we beguile 40
The lazy time, if not with some delight?
   Phil. There is a brief how many sports are ripe:
Make choice of which your highness will see first.
                          [*Giving a paper*
   The. [*Reads*] 'The battle with the Centaurs, to be sung
By an Athenian singer to the harp.'   45

We'll none of that: that have I told my love,
In glory of my kinsman Hercules.
[*Reads*] 'The riot of the tipsy Bacchanals,
Tearing the Thracian singer in their rage.'

That is an old device; and it was play'd   50
When I from Thebes came last a conqueror.
[*Reads*] 'The thrice three Muses mourning for the death
Of Learning, late deceased in beggary.'

That is some satire, keen and critical,
Not sorting with a nuptial ceremony.   55
|*Reads*] 'A tedious brief scene of young Pyramus
And his love Thisbe; very tragical mirth.'

Merry and tragical! tedious and brief!
That is, hot ice and wondrous strange snow.
How shall we find the concord of this discord?   60

    Phil. A play there is, my lord, some ten words
      long,
Which is as brief as I have known a play;
But by ten words, my lord, it is too long,
Which makes it tedious; for in all the play
There is not one word apt, one player fitted: 65
And tragical, my noble lord, it is;
For Pyramus therein doth kill himself.
Which, when I saw rehearsed, I must confess,
Made mine eyes water; but more merry tears
The passion of loud laughter never shed.   70

    The. What are they that do play it?

    Phil. Hard-handed men that work in Athens here,
Which never labour'd in their minds till now,
And now have toil'd their unbreathed memories
With this same play, against your nuptial.   75

    The. And we will hear it.

    Phil.   No, my noble lord;
It is not for you: I have heard it over,
And it is nothing, nothing in the world;
Unless you can find sport in their intents,
Extremely stretch'd and conn'd with cruel pain,   80
To do you service.

    The.   I will hear that play;
For never anything can be amiss,
When simpleness and duty tender it.
Go, bring them in: and take your places, ladies.
                              [Exit Philostrate

    Hip. I love not to see wretchedness o'ercharged   85
And duty in his service perishing.

    The. Why, gentle sweet, you shall see no such
      thing.

    Hip. He says they can do nothing in this kind.

The. The kinder we, to give them thanks for no-
  thing.
Our sport shall be to take what they mistake: 90
And what poor duty would, but cannot do,
Noble respect takes it in might, not merit.
Where I have come, great clerks have purposed
To greet me with premeditated welcomes;
Where I have seen them shiver and look pale,   95
Make periods in the midst of sentences,
Throttle their practised accent in their fears
And in conclusion dumbly have broke off,
Not paying me a welcome. Trust me, sweet,
Out of this silence yet I pick'd a welcome;   100
And in the modesty of fearful duty
I read as much as from the rattling tongue
Of saucy and audacious eloquence.
Love, therefore, and tongue-tied simplicity
In least speak most, to my capacity.   105

Re-enter PHILOSTRATE

Phil. So please your grace, the Prologue is address'd.
The. Let him approach.   [*Flourish of trumpets*

Enter QUINCE *for the* Prologue

Pro. If we offend, it is with our good will.
    That you should think, we come not to offend,
  But with good will. To show our simple skill,   110
    That is the true beginning of our end.
  Consider then we come but in despite.
    We do not come as minding to content you,
  Our true intent is. All for your delight
    We are not here. That you should here repent you,   115
  The actors are at hand and by their show
  You shall know all that you are like to know.

The. This fellow doth not stand upon points.
Lys. He hath rid his prologue like a rough colt; he

knows not the stop. A good moral, my lord: it is not 120
enough to speak, but to speak true.

Hip. Indeed he hath played on his prologue like a
child on a recorder; a sound, but not in government.

The. His speech was like a tangled chain; nothing
impaired, but all disordered. Who is next?   125

Enter PYRAMUS *and* THISBE, WALL, MOONSHINE, *and*
LION

Pro. Gentles, perchance you wonder at this show;
 But wonder on, till truth make all things plain.
This man is Pyramus, if you would know;
 This beauteous lady Thisby is certáin.
This man, with lime and rough-cast, doth present   130
 Wall, that vile Wall which did these lovers sunder;
And through Wall's chink, poor souls, they are content
 To whisper. At the which let no man wonder.
This man, with lanthorn, dog, and bush of thorn,
 Presenteth Moonshine; for, if you will know,   135
By moonshine did these lovers think no scorn
 To meet at Ninus' tomb, there, there to woo.
This grisly beast, which Lion hight by name,
 The trusty Thisby, coming first by night,
Did scare away, or rather did affright;   140
 And, as she fled, her mantle she did fall,
Which Lion vile with bloody mouth did stain.
 Anon comes Pyramus, sweet youth and tall,
And finds his trusty Thisby's mantle slain:
 Whereat, with blade, with bloody blameful blade,   145
He bravely broach'd his boiling bloody breast;
 And Thisby, tarrying in mulberry shade,
His dagger drew, and died. For all the rest,
Let Lion, Moonshine, Wall, and lovers twain
At large discourse, while here they do remain.   150
   [*Exeunt Prologue, Pyramus, Thisbe, Lion,
    and Moonshine*

The. I wonder if the lion be to speak.

Dem. No wonder, my lord: one lion may, when
many asses do.

Wall. In this same interlude it doth befall
    That I, one Snout by name, present a wall;   155
    And such a wall, as I would have you think,
    That had in it a crannied hole or chink,
    Through which the lovers, Pyramus and Thisby,
    Did whisper often very secretly.
    This loam, this rough-cast, and this stone doth show 160
    That I am that same wall; the truth is so:
    And this the cranny is, right and sinister,
    Through which the fearful lovers are to whisper.

The. Would you desire lime and hair to speak better?

Dem. It is the wittiest partition that ever I heard 165
discourse, my lord.

Re-enter PYRAMUS

The. Pyramus draws near the wall: silence.

Pyr. O grim-look'd night! O night with hue so black!
    O night, which ever art when day is not!
    O night, O night! alack, alack, alack,   170
    I fear my Thisby's promise is forgot!
    And thou, O wall, O sweet, O lovely wall,
    That stand'st between her father's ground and mine!
    Thou wall, O wall, O sweet and lovely wall,
    Show me thy chink, to blink through with mine eyne! 175
                      [Wall holds up his fingers
    Thanks, courteous wall: Jove shield thee well for this!
    But what see I? No Thisby do I see.
    O wicked wall, through whom I see no bliss!
    Cursed be thy stones for thus deceiving me!

The. The wall, methinks, being sensible, should 180
curse again.

Pyr. No, in truth, sir, he should not. 'Deceiving
me' is Thisby's cue: she is to enter now, and I am to
spy her through the wall. You shall see, it will fall
pat as I told you. Yonder she comes.   185

Re-enter THISBE

This. O wall, full often hast thou heard my moans,
    For parting my fair Pyramus and me!

       My cherry lips have often kiss'd thy stones,
         Thy stones with lime and hair knit up in thee.

Pyr. I see a voice: now will I to the chink,   190
       To spy an I can hear my Thisby's face.
       Thisby!

This.   My love! thou art my love, I think.

Pyr. Think what thou wilt, I am thy lover's grace;
       And, like Limander, am I trusty still.

This. And I like Helen, till the Fates me kill.   195

Pyr. Not Shafalus to Procrus was so true.

This. As Shafalus to Procrus, I to you.

Pyr. O, kiss me through the hole of this vile wall!

This. I kiss the wall's hole, not your lips at all.

Pyr. Wilt thou at Ninny's tomb meet me straightwáy?   200

This. 'Tide life, 'tide death, I come without delay.

               [Exeunt Pyramus and Thisbe

Wall. Thus have I, Wall, my part dischargèd so;
       And, being done, thus Wall away doth go.   *[Exit*

The. Now is the mural down between the two
neighbours.   205

Dem. No remedy, my lord, when walls are so wilful
to hear without warning.

Hip. This is the silliest stuff that ever I heard.

The. The best in this kind are but shadows; and
the worst are no worse, if imagination amend them.   210

Hip. It must be your imagination then, and not
theirs.

The. If we imagine no worse of them than they of
themselves, they may pass for excellent men.   Here
come two noble beasts in, a man and a lion.   215

Re-enter LION *and* MOONSHINE

Lion. You, ladies, you, whose gentle hearts do fear
       The smallest monstrous mouse that creeps on floor,
May now perchance both quake and tremble here,
       When lion rough in wildest rage doth roar.
Then know that I, one Snug the joiner, am   220
A lion fell, nor else no lion's dam;
For, if I should as lion come in strife
Into this place, 't were pity on my life.

The. A very gentle beast, and of a good conscience.

Dem. The very best at a beast, my lord, that ere I 225
saw.

Lys. This lion is a very fox for his valour.

The. True; and a goose for his discretion.

Dem. Not so, my lord; for his valour cannot carry
his discretion; and the fox carries the goose.   230

The. His discretion, I am sure, cannot carry his
valour; for the goose carries not the fox. It is well:
leave it to his discretion, and let us listen to the
moon.

Moon. This lanthorn doth the hornèd moon present;—   235

Dem. He should have worn the horns on his head.

The. He is no crescent, and his horns are invisible
within the circumference.

Moon. This lanthorn doth the hornèd moon present;
Myself the man i' the moon do seem to be.   240

The. This is the greatest error of all the rest: the
man should be put into the lanthorn. How is it else
the man i' the moon?

Dem. He dares not come there for the candle; for,
you see, it is already in snuff.   245

Hip. I am aweary of this moon: would he would
change!

The. It appears, by his small light of discretion,
that he is in the wane; but yet, in courtesy, in all
reason, we must stay the time.   250

Lys. Proceed, Moon.

Moon. All that I have to say is, to tell you that the
lanthorn is the moon; I, the man in the moon; this
thorn-bush, my thorn-bush; and this dog, my dog.

Dem. Why, all these should be in the lanthorn; for 255
all these are in the moon. But, silence! here comes
Thisbe.

Re-enter THISBE

This. This is old Ninny's tomb. Where is my love?
Lion. [*Roaring*] Oh——   [*Thisbe runs off*

Dem. Well roared, Lion.   26c
The. Well run, Thisbe.
Hip. Well shone, Moon. Truly, the moon shines
with a good grace.
            [*The Lion shakes Thisbe's mantle, and exit*
The. Well moused, Lion.
Lys. And so the lion vanished.   265
Dem. And then came Pyramus.

Re-enter PYRAMUS

Pyr. Sweet Moon, I thank thee for thy sunny beams;
        I thank thee, Moon, for shining now so bright;
        For, by thy gracious, golden, glittering gleams,
        I trust to take of truest Thisby sight.   270
                    But stay, O spite!
                    But mark, poor knight,
                What dreadful dole is here!
                Eyes, do you see?
                How can it be?   275
            O dainty duck! O dear!
                Thy mantle good,
                What, stain'd with blood!
            Approach, ye Furies fell!
                O Fates, come, come,   280
                Cut thread and thrum;
            Quail, crush, conclude, and quell!

The. This passion, and the death of a dear friend,
would go near to make a man look sad.

Hip. Beshrew my heart, but I pity the man.   285

Pyr. O wherefore, Nature, didst thou lions frame?
        Since lion vile hath here deflower'd my dear:
        Which is—no, no—which was the fairest dame
        That lived, that loved, that liked, that look'd with cheer.
                Come, tears, confound;   290
                Out, sword, and wound
            The pap of Pyramus;

      Ay, that left pap,
      Where heart doth hop: *[Stabs himself*
    Thus die I, thus, thus, thus.   295
      Now am I dead,
      Now am I fled;
    My soul is in the sky:
      Tongue, lose thy light;
      Moon, take thy flight: *[Exit Moonshine* 300
    Now die, die, die, die, die.   *[Dies*

Dem. No die, but an ace, for him; for he is but
one.

Lys. Less than an ace, man; for he is dead; he is
nothing.   305

The. With the help of a surgeon he might yet re-
cover, and prove an ass.

Hip. How chance Moonshine is gone before Thisbe
comes back and finds her lover?

The. She will find him by starlight. Here she comes; 310
and her passion ends the play.

Re-enter THISBE

Hip. Methinks she should not use a long one for
such a Pyramus: I hope she will be brief.

Dem. A mote will turn the balance, which Pyramus,
which Thisbe, is the better; he for a man, God war- 315
rant us; she for a woman, God bless us.

Lys. She hath spied him already with those sweet
eyes.

Dem. And thus she means, videlicet:—

    This. Asleep, my love?   320
      What, dead, my dove?
    O Pyramus, arise!
      Speak, speak. Quite dumb?
      Dead, dead? A tomb
    Must cover thy sweet eyes.   325
      These lily lips,
      This cherry nose,
    These yellow cowslip cheeks,

Are gone, are gone:
Lovers, make moan: 330
His eyes were green as leeks.
O Sisters Three,
Come, come to me,
With hands as pale as milk;
Lay them in gore,   335
Since you have shore
With shears his thread of silk.
Tongue, not a word:
Come, trusty sword;
Come, blade, my breast imbrue: [*Stabs herself* 340
And, farewell, friends;
Thus Thisby ends:
Adieu, adieu, adieu.   [*Dies*

The. Moonshine and Lion are left to bury the dead.
Dem. Ay, and Wall too.   345
Bot. [*Starting up*] No, I assure you; the wall is down
that parted their fathers. Will it please you to see the
epilogue, or to hear a Bergomask dance between two of
our company?

The. No epilogue, I pray you: for your play needs no 350
excuse. Never excuse; for when the players are all
dead, there need none to be blamed. Marry, if he that
writ it had played Pyramus and hanged himself in
Thisbe's garter, it would have been a fine tragedy:
and so it is, truly; and very notably discharged. But 355
come, your Bergomask: let your epilogue alone.

[*A dance*

The iron tongue of midnight hath told twelve:
Lovers, to bed; 'tis almost fairy time.
I fear we shall out-sleep the coming morn
As much as we this night have overwatch'd.   360
This palpable-gross play hath well beguiled
The heavy gait of night. Sweet friends, to bed.
A fortnight hold we this solemnity,
In nightly revels and new jollity.

[*Exeunt*

A Dance.—(Act v. 1, 356.)

Enter PUCK

Puck. Now the hungry lion roars,   365
    And the wolf behowls the moon;
Whilst the heavy ploughman snores,
    All with weary task fordone.
Now the wasted brands do glow,
    Whilst the screech-owl, screeching loud,   370
Puts the wretch that lies in woe
    In remembrance of a shroud.
Now it is the time of night
    That the graves all gaping wide,
Every one lets forth his sprite,   375
    In the church-way paths to glide:
And we fairies, that do run
    By the triple Hecate's team,
From the presence of the sun,
    Following darkness like a dream,   380
Now are frolic: not a mouse
Shall disturb this hallow'd house:
I am sent with broom before,
To sweep the dust behind the door.

Enter OBERON *and* TITANIA *with their train*

Obe. Through the house give glimmering light,   385
    By the dead and drowsy fire:
Every elf and fairy sprite
    Hop as light as bird from brier;
And this ditty, after me,
Sing, and dance it trippingly.   390
Tita. First, rehearse your song by rote,
    To each word a warbling note:
Hand in hand, with fairy grace,
We will sing, and bless this place.

                [*Song and dance*

Obe. Now, until the break of day,   395
    Through this house each fairy stray.

To the best bride-bed will we,
Which by us shall blessed be;
So shall all the couples three
Ever true in loving be;   400
And the blots of Nature's hand
Shall not in their issue stand;
Never mole, hare-lip, nor scar,
Nor mark prodigious, such as are
Despisèd in nativity,   405
Shall upon their children be.
With this field-dew consecrate,
Every fairy take his gait;
And each several chamber bless,
Through this palace, with sweet peace;   410
And the owner of it blest
Ever shall in safety rest.
Trip away; make no stay;
Meet me all by break of day.
                    [*Exeunt Oberon, Titania, and train*
Puck. If we shadows have offended,   415
Think but this, and all is mended,
That you have but slumber'd here,
While these visions did appear.
And this weak and idle theme,
No more yielding but a dream.   420
Gentles, do not reprehend:
If you pardon, we will mend:
And, as I am an honest Puck,
If we have unearned luck
Now to 'scape the serpent's tongue,   425
We will make amends ere long;
Else the Puck a liar call:
So, good night unto you all.
Give me your hands, if we be friends,
And Robin shall restore amends.   [*Exit* 430

To the best bride-bed will we,
Which by us shall blessed be;
So shall all the couples three
Ever true in loving be;
And the blots of Nature's hand
Shall not in their issue stand;
Never mole, hare-lip, nor scar,
Nor mark prodigious, such as are
Despised in nativity,
Shall upon their children be.
With this field-dew consecrate,
Every fairy take his gait;
And each several chamber bless,
Through this palace, with sweet peace;
And the owner of it blest
Ever shall in safety rest.
Trip away; make no stay;
Meet me all by break of day.

[*Exeunt Oberon, Titania, and train.*

Puck. If we shadows have offended,
Think but this, and all is mended,
That you have but slumber'd here
While these visions did appear.
And this weak and idle theme,
No more yielding but a dream,
Gentles, do not reprehend:
If you pardon, we will mend:
And, as I am an honest Puck,
If we have unearned luck
Now to 'scape the serpent's tongue,
We will make amends ere long;
Else the Puck a liar call:
So, good night unto you all.
Give me your hands, if we be friends,
And Robin shall restore amends.

[*Exit.*

NOTES

Act I—Scene 1

1. **nuptial hour,** wedding hour. (Lat. *nubeo, nupsi, nuptum,* to marry.)

3. **methinks,** it seems to me. An impersonal verb.

4. **she lingers my desires,** she delays the accomplishment of my desires.

5. **step-dame,** step-mother. (O.E. *steop,* Ger. *stief.*)

dowager, a widow who has a dowage or dowry from an estate. (Fr. *douer,* to endow.)

7-11. 'The day will quickly end in night, and the nights will pass rapidly in dreams. When four days and nights shall have so passed our wedding will take place.'

11. **solemnities,** the festivities to take place on the solemnization of our wedding. A solemnity originally meant something which took place every year. (Oscan, *sollus,* every; Lat. *annus,* a year.)

Philostrate. Pronounce in three syllables; for Philostratus.

15. **companion,** fellow, used contemptuously. Originally, one who ate with another. (Lat. *cum,* with, *panis,* bread.) *Fellow* and *companion* have exchanged meanings since Shakespeare's time.

19. **With pomp, with triumph.** A triumph was a solemn procession in which a victorious Roman general entered the city in a chariot drawn by four horses. *Pomp* is from a Greek word having much the same signification.

20. **duke.** From the Lat. *dux,* a leader. Chaucer gives this title to Theseus, but in Grecian history he is called king.

21. **Egeus.** Pronounce in three syllables.

what's the news with thee? what has happened to thee?

32. 'Impressed your image on her imagination, or gained her love by stealth.'

fantasy, fancy, which then meant 'liking' or 'love'.

33. **gawds** (or *gauds*), trifling ornaments, toys. (Lat. *gaudium,* joy.)

conceits, fanciful devices.

34. **Knacks,** trinkets, toys. (Ger. *Knack,* a snap with the fingers; then 'a trifle'.)

35. 'Having strong influence with tender youth.'

99

36. **filch'd**, stolen.

39. 'If it be so that she will not', &c.

your grace, a term applied formerly to the sovereign of England as to one from whom *favours* were to be had (Lat. *gratia*, a favour); now used to dukes and archbishops.

41, 42. Solon, the Athenian lawgiver who was born long after the time of Theseus, gave this power to fathers. Fathers had the power of life and death over their children in Rome also.

41. **privilege of Athens**, rights enjoyed by Athenians.

45. 'Expressly provided to meet such a case as this.'

46. **be advised**, be careful, take care, consider.

50, 51. 'It is in his power to leave the figure as it is, or to obliterate it.'

54. 'But in this respect, viz. that he is without your father's consent.'

60, 61. 'Nor how far it is befitting to my modesty to express my thoughts, in the presence of such as are here.'

65, 66. 'Either to die the death appointed for such an offence, or to give up for ever the society of men.'

68. 'Enquire of your youthfulness, examine well your passions.'

69. **Whether**, to be pronounced 'where', as it is still in many parts of the country.

70, 71. 'You can bear the condition denoted by the dress of a nun, and be shut up for ever in a shady cloister.' The words *nun* and *cloister* belong to the monastic life in Roman Catholic countries, but in ancient times maidens became priestesses in the temple of Diana, the virgin-goddess (*e.g.* Iphigenia, the daughter of Agamemnon).

70. **livery**, now applied to the dress of servants. It was formerly any distinctive costume. Here used for the condition or state implied by the dress.

71. **aye**, ever. (O.E. *a* or *ava*, ever, always.)

cloister, a religious house. (Lat. *claudo*, I shut; Ger. *Kloster*.)

mew'd, shut up as in a mue or coop, where the falcons were put to *mue* or *moult* their feathers.

72. **sister**, nun.

73. The moon was the type of chastity, as being under the control of Diana, the moon-goddess, sister of Apollo, the sun-god.

74, 75. 'Thrice blessed are they who control their passions so as to endure a life of virginity.'
Elizabeth was unmarried, and nothing pleased her more than to hear praises of a single life.

76-78. 'Yet as far as earthly bliss is concerned, the rose from which the perfume is extracted is happier than one which withers on the bush.'
This is a poetical way of saying that a married life is preferable to a single one.

80. **virgin patent,** the privileges to which, as a maiden, I am entitled. A patent is a privilege from the crown granted by "letters patent", or a document open to the perusal of all. (Lat. *pateo*, I lie open.)

81, 82. 'Unto the sovereignty of that man to whose yoke my soul is unwilling to give supreme power.'
Note the omission of 'to' before 'whose'.

84, 85. 'The day on which my love and I shall seal a bond of everlasting companionship', *i.e.* be married.

92. **crazed title,** a title in which there is a flaw; a weak title. (Either from the Greek *keraso*, to dilute, and so weaken, or the Swedish *krasa*, to crush.)

96. **render,** give, bestow upon.

98. **estate,** make over as an estate.

99–102. 'I am descended from as good ancestors, and am as well off. My love is greater than his. In every way my fortunes are equal, if not superior, to those of Demetrius.'

106. **avouch it to his head,** assert it to his face.

109. **dotes in idolatry,** dotes even to idolatry.

110. **spotted,** wicked, defiled. Lit. with spots and blemishes; opposed to spotless, without spots.

112. **spoke,** for 'spoken'. This form is often used by Shakespeare for the past participle.

113. **self-affairs,** my own affairs. Words compounded with *self* are very common in Shakespeare. They are comparatively rare now. (Self-esteem, self-respect.)

116. **schooling,** instructions.

120. **extenuate,** diminish the force of. (Lat. *extenuo*, to make thin.)

122. **what cheer?** how are you feeling? how do you fare?
(The French *chère*, fare, is from the Low Latin *cara*, a countenance.)

129. **How chance.** 'How does it chance or happen.'

131. **Beteem,** pour upon.

132. **Ay me!** equivalent to 'Ah, me!' an exclamation of pain or weariness. *Me* is dative.

   for aught, from all.

135. **in blood,** in rank or position.

136. 'Oh vexation for (a marriage to be forbidden because) one is too high in rank to be subjected to one in a low position.'

137. **misgraffed,** wrongly grafted—as buds on the wrong tree. (Fr. *greffer*, to graft.)

141–143. 'Or, if the choice was mutually agreeable and suitable, war, death, or sickness attacked it and made it as momentary as a sound, as swift as a shadow.'

145. **collied,** blackened. In the western counties 'colly' is the soot on pots and kettles.

146. **in a spleen,** by a sudden movement, as in anger.

149. **confusion;** in four syllables.

151. **edict',** accent on the second syllable. (Lat. *edictum*, a decree.)

152. **patience;** in three syllables.

153. 'Because it is a vexation which belongs to love as much as dreams and sighs, wishes and tears, the usual followers of poor Love.

156. **A good persuasion,** a good argument.

157. **a widow aunt.** The more usual expression would be 'a widowed aunt'. (Lat. *vidua*, deprived of, *i.e.* a husband.)

158. **revénue.** Note the accent.

160. **respects,** regards or looks upon.

167. **To do observance to a morn of May,** to observe the rites or ceremonies of May-day. Festivities in honour of Flora, the goddess of flowers, were instituted by Romulus, the founder of Rome, and lasted from April 28th to May 3rd. Later, they were observed annually. Similar festivities were perhaps held in honour of the Greek goddess Chloris. The ancient Britons and early English paid great respect to May-day as the birthday of the flowers. The ceremony of bringing in the May in the early morning, crowning the May-queen, and dancing round the May-pole were long observed in this country. They seem now to have almost died out.

169. **Cupid,** the son of Venus, was the god of Love. Some of his arrows were tipped with gold, others with lead. The former inspired love, the latter repelled it.

171. **simplicity,** innocence.

The chariot of Venus, the goddess of Love and Beauty, was drawn by doves.

172. **prospers,** makes prosperous. 'To prosper' is generally an intransitive verb.

173, 174. Æneas, in his flight from Troy, visited Carthage, lately founded by Dido, a fugitive from Tyre, and was well received and entertained. The queen fell in love with her guest, and he promised her marriage. She burnt herself on a funeral pyre, when she saw his ships sailing away from Carthage.
This is an anachronism, Dido and Æneas having lived many years after Theseus.

175, 176. **broke** and **spoke,** for 'broken' and 'spoken'.

182. 'Demetrius loves your fairness (beauty), O happy fair one!'

183. **lode-stars,** leading-stars. The Polar star is so called because it *leads* sailors.

184. **tuneable,** tuneful.

186. **catching,** contagious or infectious. In the next three lines Helena uses the word *catch* in the sense of *catch hold of*, *i.e.* get possession of.

186. **favour,** beauty.

190, 191. 'If all the world were mine, I would give you everything to be transformed into your likeness, with the exception of Demetrius.'

194-201. This line-for-line dialogue is a characteristic of Shakespeare's early plays.

201. 'His folly is caused by no fault of yours, except your beauty.'

204-207. 'Before she saw Lysander, her mind was tranquil and at peace, and therefore Athens seemed a paradise. But the agitation and anxiety produced by her love, and her father's opposition to it, altogether changed the character of the place. What power must there then be in Lysander's charms to cause such a change of feeling!'

209. **Phœbe**, the name of Diana in her capacity as goddess of the moon, and so applied to the moon itself. Apollo, when driving the chariot of the sun, was called Phœbus. Both names are from a Greek word, meaning *bright*.

209-213. 'We have planned to steal through the gates of Athens, when Phœbe sees her silver-like countenance in the mirror formed by the water, adorning the blades of grass with dewdrops—a time which always conceals lovers' flights.

215. **faint primrose-beds**; either beds of faint-smelling primroses, or of pale primroses.

219. **stranger companies**, companies of strangers.

222, 223. 'Keep your word, Lysander; we must not see each other until midnight to-morrow.'

225. 'As you dote on Demetrius, so may he dote on you.'

226. 'How happy some people can be in comparison with others.'

other some = lit. a second some: another body of people.

230-233. 'And just as he errs in doting on Hermia's eyes, so do I in admiring his qualities. Love can transform things which are base and common, and make them appear beautiful and dignified out of all proportion to their deserts.'

235. Cupid's being blind is a comparatively modern idea. He is not so represented in ancient times.

236-239. 'Nor has the mind of Love a particle of judgment. Wings and no eyes typify unreasoning haste. And Love is said to be a child for this reason, because he is so often deceived.'

240. 'As playful boys break their oaths in sport, so the boy Love breaks his everywhere.'

242. **eyne**, the old English plural of eye. (Cf. 'oxen', 'children'.)

243-245. 'He poured down oaths as thick as hail, that he was only mine; but when he felt love for Hermia, the heat of this passion dissolved his love for me, just as hail is melted by heat.'

249-251. 'If I have thanks it will be dearly purchased (as he and Hermia will meet). But I shall be recompensed for this pain, by his company, or at any rate by the sight of him thither and back again.'

Act I—Scene 2

2. 'It would be best for you to call them separately, man by man, according to the written list.'—Note that *you* is dative.

generally, a ridiculous mistake of Bottom's: he means the opposite, 'separately'. Shakespeare often raises a laugh by such means as this, in his earlier plays especially.

4. The antecedent of **which** is 'every man': note the use of 'which' with persons. Note also the intentional opposition of 'wedding-*day*' and 'night'. See previous note.

5. **interlude,** a short entertainment given in the intervals of a festival. (Lat. *inter*, between; *ludere*, to play.)

9. **on** = of.

11. **Marry,** a mild form of oath from the name of the Virgin Mary. It signifies 'indeed', 'certainly', 'well then', &c.

lamentable comedy, a contradiction in terms, probably in ridicule of the titles of some plays then in vogue.

21. The chief character in the plays before Shakespeare's time was the noisy, swaggering tyrant. Herod the Great was a favourite, and was made to rant all kinds of nonsense. (See Longfellow's *Golden Legend.*)

26. **condole,** mourn, lament. (The literal and only modern meaning is to grieve *with*, or express sympathy with another's sorrow: Lat. *con*, with; *dolere*, to mourn.)

26, 27. **in some measure,** in some considerable measure.

27. **humour,** whim, fancy.

28. **Ercles,** Greek *Heracles*, Roman *Hercules*. A celebrated demi-god, whose life on earth was a series of thrilling adventures. These were favourite subjects for the drama before Shakespeare's time. Hercules is generally represented as a blusterer, such as Bottom would delight in.

28, 29. **to tear a cat, to make all split,** proverbial expressions for ranting, blustering.

34. **Phibbus,** Phœbus, the Sun-god.

44. **a wandering knight.** Wandering knights or knights-errant were men who wandered about in search of abuses. Cervantes, who died within a few days of Shakespeare, wrote *Don Quixote* in ridicule of them.

46. **play a woman.** Women's parts (in public) were generally played by boys before the Restoration. The first important character played by a woman was Desdemona in Shakespeare's *Othello*, in the reign of Charles II.

48. **That's all one.** (Ger. *Das ist mir einerlei*, *lit.* that is of one kind to me.)

play it in a mask. This was usual when the man cast for the woman's part had an especially masculine appearance.

50. Notice how anxious Bottom is to play *all* the leading parts: cf. line 69.

50. **An**, if, a shorter form of the Scandinavian 'and'=if. And if=if if, a reduplication.

51, 52. **Thisne, Thisne.** This is either the result of Bottom's first attempt to render 'Thisbe' in a "monstrous little voice", or it may be a corruption of a country expression *thissen*, in this way.

57. The programme as here arranged was not carried out. Changes were made during the rehearsal later on.

Starveling. Shakespeare always speaks slightingly of the tailor's calling. Here he suggests that it is a trade to *starve*, not to live by.

67. **extempore**, at the time, on the spur of the moment. (Lat. *ex*, out of; *tempore*, time.)

79. **discretion.** Probably Bottom means some such word as 'option' or 'choice'.

aggravate, lit. make greater. But the speaker is Bottom, who is sure to say the opposite of what he means.

81. **roar you.** The *you* is simply a colloquial insertion. It is properly = for you; = ethic dative.

83. **proper**, handsome.

86, 87. **were I best.** The original phrase was impersonal, 'me were best', in which *me* was dative. But from the analogy of 'you were best', it was supposed that the nominative ought to be used.

89. **discharge**, perform.

your, colloquial: see 'you' in line 81.

90. **purple - in - grain.** 'Purple' mentioned by Shakespeare was scarlet.

in grain, in dye. The cochineal insect from which scarlet dye was originally obtained was called *granum*.

91. **French-crown-colour**, the colour of the French gold crown-piece.

93. **French crowns.** Here 'crown' means the crown of the head. Bald heads were nicknamed French crowns, from being caused by a complaint called French disease.

96. **con**, learn so as to know thoroughly. (O.E. *cunnan*, Ger. *kennen*, to know.)

100. **draw a bill of properties**, write out a list of articles required.

104. **obscenely**, perhaps 'obscurely', 'darkly'.

107. **hold or cut bow-strings**, keep your appointment, or give up the affair. An expression used by archers in making an engagement. If they did not hold, or keep, their appointment, their friends might cut their bow-strings.

Act II—Scene 1

3. **Thorough**, through; so pronounced for the sake of the metre.

7. **moonës.** The apostrophe was rarely if ever used in Shakespeare's time. In the original text this word is spelt 'moons', and was no doubt pronounced as two syllables. Cf. iv. 1. 96, where 'nights' before 'shade' is probably to be pronounced 'nightës'.

7. **sphere,** orbit, *i.e.* the space through which the moon makes its circuit, and which was supposed to move as well as the moon. Or it may mean the moon itself. (Gr. *sphaira,* a sphere, or globe.)

9. **orbs,** the circles of grass known as fairy rings, which were supposed to be caused by fairies dancing in a ring.

10. **The cowslips tall her pensioners be.** The guards of Henry VIII and Elizabeth were called pensioners from the payment they received (Lat. *pensio,* a payment), and wore splendid dresses ornamented with gold lace.

12. **fairy favours,** gifts of the fairies.

13. ' In these spots their fragrance abides.' The spots of the cowslip are inside the bell.

14. **dewdrops.** Dewdrops are often called pearls by the poets.

16. **thou lob of spirits,** thou lout among spirits. *Lob* is akin to the Ger. *Lapp* or *Lump,* meaning anything clumsy or loutish. Puck was not so dainty a sprite as Titania and her attendants. His dealings were mostly with homely people.

17. **elves,** fairies (Ger. *Elf,* a fairy).

anon, immediately. (O.E. *on,* in; *an,* one = in one (instant).)

20. **passing fell and wrath,** exceedingly fierce and angry. (O.E. *fell,* bad.)

22. **stolen,** pronounce *stoln.*

23. **changeling.** It was a common superstition that fairies carried off babies and left others in their places. The child left was generally called the changeling. In this case it was the one taken away. *Changeling* here is in three syllables.

28. **they,** *i.e.* Oberon and Titania.

29. **sheen,** brightness; that which shines. It may possibly be an adjective here.

30. **square,** quarrel. (Fr. *se quereller,* to quarrel; *se carrer,* to strut.)

31. **them,** themselves.

33. **shrewd sprite,** mischievous spirit.

35. **villagery,** the village and all appertaining to it.

36. **quern,** a hand-mill for grinding corn. As this machine and a churn were worked in the same way, it is possible that Shakespeare wrote *quern* instead of, and at the same time to rime with ' churn '. Both the skimming of the milk and Puck working in the churn would make the labour fruitless.

37. **bootless,** without profit. (O.E. *bote,* a compensation.)

38. **sometime,** sometimes.

barm, the ' head ' or workings out of beer. The word is still used in many country districts. (O.E. *beorme,* yeast.)

39. **Mislead,** in the shape of the ignis fatuus or Will o' the Wisp.

laughing at their harm, laughing at the harm which happens to them.

40. **Hobgoblin,** for 'Robgoblin'. *Rob* = Robin. *Goblin* from the Latin *gobelinus*, a sprite.

46. **filly foal,** young mare. (Ice. *fyl*, a foal.)

47. **gossip's bowl,** a beverage compounded of ale, nutmeg, sugar, toast, and roasted crab-apples, in great favour at christening parties.

Gossip is a corruption of 'Godsib' (*God*, and *sib*, a relationship), and was given to sponsors in baptism. As a great deal of conversation attended the proceedings subsequent to a christening, the word *gossip* was applied to any talkative person.

48. **crab,** crab-apple, a wild sour apple. (Ger. *herb*, Lat. *acerbus*, sour.)

50. **dewlap,** the loose skin which hangs from the neck of cattle. Here used for the neck itself.

51. **The wisest aunt,** the old woman who thinks herself the wisest of the party. In some parts of the country aunt is used as a term of familiarity, without implying relationship.

52. **three-foot,** three-legged. Note the omission of the article.

54. **And 'tailor' cries.** The only explanation suggested for the custom is Dr. Johnson's: "The custom of crying 'tailor' at a sudden fall backwards, I think I remember to have observed. He that slips beside his chair, falls as a tailor squats upon his board." It is possible, however, that the word 'tailor' was used as a term of reproach, just as its German equivalent is now. "You Schneider" would be applied by many people in London now to a person pulling a chair from under them, or performing any similar trick.

55. **quire,** the whole party in chorus.

56. **waxen in their mirth,** increase in their mirth, grow merrier and merrier. (Cf. Ger. *wachsen*. The *-en* in 'waxen' is a remnant of the 3rd person plural termination in the midland dialect.)

    neeze, sneeze.

64–68. 'I know of occasions when thou hast stolen away from fairy-land, and sat all day in the shape of Corin, playing on pipes made of corn-stalks, and making love in verses to amorous Phillida.' **Corin,** a poetical name for a shepherd; **Phillida,** or Phillis, for a shepherdess. 'Phillida' is properly the accusative case.

69. **Come,** having come.

    steppe. It is probable that Shakespeare meant to write *steep*, as the word *steppe*, a plain, was unknown in England in his time. The *steeps* of India would be the precipitous places of that country.

70. **bouncing Amazon.** Hippolyta was queen of the Amazons, a race of warlike women who had a kingdom in Asia Minor.

Bouncing was said of a woman, where 'swaggering' or 'strutting' would be said of a man.

71. **buskin'd,** a participle formed from a noun. The 'buskin' was a kind of half-boot with high heels, worn by persons hunting, and also by actors. (O.F. *brossequin*.) Hippolyta was a great huntress, as were all the Amazons.

72. **must be**, is on the point of being; = French, *doit être*.

75. **Glance at**, hint at.

   credit, influence, depending on good opinion.

79. **Ariadne** was the daughter of Minos, king of Crete. She ex-plained to Theseus the mystery of the labyrinth, in return for which he married her, but left her in the island of Naxos.

   Antiopa was either the mother or the sister of Hippolyta.

80. **forgeries**, inventions, acts of imagination.

81. **middle summer's spring**, the 'spring' or beginning of midsummer. There is no reference to the season 'spring', which derives its name from the fact that then vegetation begins to 'spring'.

83. **paved fountain**, fountain with a pebbly bottom.

84. **in the beached margent of the sea**, on the margin or edge of the sea, formed by the beach.

85. 'To dance in circles to the music of the whistling wind.'

89. **Contagious**, pestilential.

90. **pelting**, paltry, petty, insignificant. The derivation of the word is not certain.

91. **they**, the rivers.

   their continents, the banks which contained them. (Lat. *con*, to-gether; *teneo*, I hold.)

92–96. Notice this picture of ruin in the country side, and how much is expressed in how few words: especially notice the force of the epithet *murrion* (now spelt 'murrain', and no longer used as an adjective).

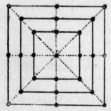

97. **nine men's morris**, called also nine men's merrils, 'merrils' being the French name for the counters with which it was played. It was an outdoor game of draughts, common in Warwickshire and Northamptonshire. The board was cut out in the grass in three con-centric squares, a hole being cut in the corner of each square, one in the middle of each side, and one in the common centre. Two players having nine counters or merrils each, placed one of these alternately in a hole, the aim of his opponent being to prevent his getting three in a line (cf. 'Noughts and Crosses'). In wet weather the holes would be filled up. The game was also called 'five-penny morris'.

98. **And the quaint mazes in the wanton green**, *i.e.* the fanciful turnings on the luxuriant grass, intricate figures formed by constant running over the same track upon grass. *Running the figure of eight* was the most common of these; the players having to reach certain points under specified penalties. (Cf. 'rounders'.)

100–101. 'Here (round about us) men are without their usual winter: no hymns, no carols are heard at night.' The custom of singing carols at night, especially about Christmas time, is of great age.

102. **Therefore,** because of our quarrel.

the governess of floods, the moon which governs the tide, and by the appearance of which the weather can be forecast, a *pale* moon denoting coming rain.

104. **rheumatic diseases.** (Gr. *rheuma*, a flowing.) Accent *rheumatic* on the first syllable.

105. **thorough this distemperature,** through this quarrel between you and me.

108. **old Hiems,** winter personified. (Lat. *hiems*, winter.)

111. **childing,** productive.

111–113. 'Change their accustomed dress, and the bewildered world, judging each season by what it produces, cannot tell which is which.'

114. **progeny of evils,** family of evils.

115. **debate,** quarrel. **dissension,** four syllables.

116. **original,** origin, or original cause.

120. **henchman,** page. The derivation of this word is uncertain. It is most probably a corruption of *hengst-man*, a horseman or groom. (O.E. *hengest*, a horse.)

121. 'I would not sell the child for all fairy-land.'

122. **votaress,** a woman who has taken a vow. The masculine form is 'votary'. (Lat. *voveo, votum*, to vow.)

125. **Neptune,** god of the sea.

130. **intend you stay?** Do you intend to stay? The 'to', which cannot now be omitted, was originally the sign of the gerund and not of the infinitive.

133. **go with us.** The verb 'go' is often used in the same way as the French verb *aller*, e.g. *Allons-nous-en!* 'Come on!' or 'Let us go!'

137. **chide,** quarrel.

138. **thou shalt not.** Thou shalt not go. This was a common idiom in Shakespeare's time (cf. 'This shall to the Duke').

139. **injury** has here the meaning of 'insult', like the French *injure*. (Lat. *injuria*.)

141. **Since,** when.

142. **mermaid.** Mermaids were fabulous sea-animals having the upper part of a woman and the lower part of a fish. Their singing was very beautiful. (Fr. *mer*, Lat. *mare*, the sea.)

dolphin, a species of whale, from 8 to 10 feet long. Dolphins were believed to be very fond of music: they sported around the ship that was bearing the Greek singer Arion, for example.

143. **dulcet and harmonious breath,** sweet and harmonious notes.

145. **spheres,** orbits.

146. **To hear** may perhaps mean 'at hearing', 'as they heard'. Shakespeare often uses what we should call the infinitive in this gerundial way; and then the shooting of the stars will be the *result* of the music, just as the calming of the sea is.

142-146. The 'mermaid' mentioned here is supposed by some critics to refer to Mary, Queen of Scots, whose return to Scotland calmed that turbulent country for a time. The 'Dolphin' suggests the Dauphin of France, whose wife Mary had been. The 'Stars' which shot madly from their spheres were said to refer to the Duke of Norfolk, and the Earls of Northumberland and Westmorland, who espoused the cause of Mary against Elizabeth. It is more probable that the scene was suggested by the sports given at Kenilworth by the Earl of Leicester to Elizabeth, and which Shakespeare may have seen.

147. but thou couldst not, being only an inferior sprite.

148. cold moon, chaste Diana.

149. Cupid all arm'd, Cupid with all his usual weapons. This was perhaps the Earl of Leicester, who hoped to marry Elizabeth, and gave a great entertainment in her honour at Kenilworth in 1575.

   certain aim, careful aim, aim deliberately directed.

150. a fair vestal. This without doubt is intended as a compliment to Elizabeth.

In ancient Rome a vestal was a virgin devoted to the service of the goddess of fire, Vesta.

   throned by the west, *i.e.* whose sway extends *throughout* the west: cf. 'by sea and land'.

153. I might, I could, I was able to.

154. watery moon, either because the moon controls the water of the sea, or because, as was then supposed, she drew up moisture from the earth.

155. votaress, Elizabeth, who had taken vows of virginity: cf. ii. 1. 122.

156. fancy-free, free from the power of love.

157. bolt, shaft or arrow.

159. Before milk-white. In the story of Pyramus and Thisbe, the mulberry is said to have changed colour. Shakespeare probably got the idea of the pansy's change from this.

160. love-in-idleness, one of the names of the Pansy. (Fr. *pensée*, thought.) This flower is also called heart's-ease, cull-me-to-you, three-faces-in-one-hood. 'Love-in-idleness' should be 'live-in-idleness'.

163. or . . . or, either . . . or. Common in poetry.

164. it, man or woman mentioned in the verse above.

166. leviathan, from a Hebrew word meaning an animal bent or twisted in curves. It is now generally supposed to be the crocodile.— Shakespeare called it the whale.

167. 'To put a girdle round the earth' was a common expression for making a journey round the world. Forty was used, as it is now, when any indefinite number was intended, probably from its frequent occurrence in the Bible. (Cf. 'I have told you forty times'; 'I don't care for forty such men', &c.)

174. with the soul of love, with the most intense love.

176. **another herb,** Diana's Rose or Diana's Bud.   See note in act iv. 1. 73.

182. **the other slayeth me.** He means Hermia is killing him by not returning his love.

184. **wood.** The first of these words means 'mad'. (O.E. *wód*, raging.)

187. **adamant.** It here means the lode-stone which attracts or leads iron. It generally means the diamond. (Gr. *adamos*, invincible, *i.e.* unbreakable.)

191. **speak you fair,** speak fairly or kindly to you. Cf. 'play him false'.

193. **nor I cannot.** *Nor* and *not* do not here destroy the negative, but make it more emphatic, as in Greek.

194. **even.** Pronounce *e'en.*

195. **spaniel,** a sporting dog, which is very fawning; it is so called because the breed came originally from *Spain*. (Fr. *espagnol*.)

200. **worser,** a double comparative for emphasis.

201. **of high respect,** highly respected, esteemed.

206. **impeach,** expose to reproach, charge with a crime.   The word has almost gone out of common use.   In history, persons impeached are accused by the House of Commons before the House of Lords.

209. **privilege,** protection.

   for that, because.

213. **in my respect,** in my idea, in respect or regard to me.

216. **brakes,** bushes, thickets.

219. **the story shall be changed,** the parts shall be reversed.   In Ovid's story Apollo pursued the maiden Daphne, who was changed into a laurel-bush that she might escape him.

221. **griffin,** a fabulous animal with the head, wings, and fore-legs of an eagle, and the rest of its body like a lion. (Gr. *grypos*, hook-nosed.)

   hind, female deer. (O.E. *hind*; Ger. *Hinde*.)

222. **bootless,** unavailing. (O.E. *bót*, profit.)

224. ' I will not stay to listen to your talk.'

225, 226. **do not believe But,** *i.e.* be assured that.

229. **Your wrongs,** the wrongs you do.   Helena means that it is a disgrace to a woman to woo and run after a man as she is doing; but Demetrius forces her to do so, because he will not woo her.

233. **To die,** by dying.

   upon the hand, by the hand.

239. **oxlips,** a species of cowslip with the blossoms darker and more developed.

   grows. The verb is singular here to agree with the nearer subject ' violet '.

240, 241. **Woodbine, honeysuckle; musk rose, wild rose; eglantine,** sweet-brier.

242. **sometime of the night,** sometimes at night, or during part of the night.

243. **dances and delight,** delightful dances. The use of two nouns instead of an adjective and a noun is very common in classical poetry. In grammar it is called *Hendiadys*, lit. one (idea) by two (words).

244. **throws.** Snakes shed their skins at certain periods.

245. **Weed,** dress or garment. (O.E. *waed*, a garment.) Now only used in the expression ' widow's weeds '.

246. **streak,** stroke, touch gently.

254, 255. ' Do it with great care, that he may show himself to be more deeply in love with her than she with him.'

256. **look,** take care. It was a fixed law with fairies, ghosts, &c., to go home at the first cock-crow.

Act II—Scene 2

1. **roundel,** dance in a ring.

2. **third part.** The fairies being very small, make short divisions of time.

3. **cankers,** canker-worms which prey upon buds.

4. **Some war;** subjunctive; ' *let* some *make* war '. So *some keep back* in line 5.

    rere-mice, bats (O.E. *hreran*, to move or stir). A bat is frequently called a flitter-mouse (Ger. *Fledermaus*), its body, without the wings, resembling that of the mouse.

7. **quaint,** delicate, refined. (O.F. *coint*, from Lat. *cognitus*, known; mistakenly from Lat. *comptus*, adorned.)

    asleep, ' to sleep ', as we should say.

8. **offices,** duties. (Lat. *officium*, duty.)

9–24. This song has been set to music by several composers.

9. **double tongue,** forked tongue.

10. **Thorny,** prickly.

11. **Newts and blind-worms,** called also efts (*eft* is the original word; ' *an* eft ' became ' *a* newt ') and slow-worms. Both these little creatures are quite harmless, but they are still considered poisonous in many country places.

13. **Philomel,** Philomela, an Athenian princess who was badly treated by her brother-in-law. In attempting to escape from him she was changed into a nightingale, and he into a hawk. But it is the *male* nightingale that sings.

14. **lullaby,** a song to *lull* children to sleep. (Ger. *lullen*, to lull.)

16–18. **Never harm . . . Come,** *i.e. may* harm . . . never come.

21. **spinners,** spiders, from their spinning webs. (Ger. *Spinne*, a spider.)

26. **One . . . stand,** *i.e.* let some one stand.

30. **ounce,** a lynx or small species of leopard.

    cat. Here, a wild-cat.

31. **Pard,** leopard.

36. **troth,** truth.

37. **rest us,** notice this reflexive form; the pronoun is superfluous now.

44. **Thy love ne'er alter,** may thy love never alter.

46. 'And may my life end when I end my fidelity.'

48. She does not want *all* the rest. She wishes Lysander to have half.

51. **approve,** prove or test. Puck has been sent to find Demetrius and Helena. His only direction was the Athenian dress; and as Lysander and Hermia wore it, his mistake is natural.

54. **Weeds,** see note on ii. 1. 245.

56. **Despised,** who despised.

60. **courtesy.** Pronounce *curt'sy.*

61. **Churl,** a man with rude or rough manners. (O.E. *ceorl,* a peasant.)

62. **owe,** own or possess.

63, 64. 'When thou wakest let love forbid sleep to take its seat on thy eyelids.' He means 'may love prevent you from sleeping'.

64. **his,** its. This latter word had not come into general use in Shakespeare's time.

67. **though,** even if.

69. **darkling,** in the dark.

71. **fond,** foolish, foolishly loving.

72. **the lesser is my grace,** the less favour I find. (Lat. *gratia,* favour.)

75, 76. Helena means that Hermia's eyes cannot have been made so bright by tears. For, if so, her own eyes would be still brighter than Hermia's, because she had wept more.

81. **dissembling,** deceiving.

    glass. The ancients had no looking-glasses like ours, but they made very good mirrors by polishing metal.

82. 'Made me compare (my eyes) with Hermia's star-like eyes.'

92. **What though?** what then?

97. He calls Hermia a raven because of her dark complexion. Elizabeth's hair was red, and therefore fair complexions were fashionable during her reign.

101. **ripe not,** grow not ripe, do not ripen.

102, 103. 'Having reached the highest possible point of human sagacity, my will is led by my reason.'

104. **o'erlook,** look over or read.

111. **flout,** mock at.   (Dutch *fluyten*, to jeer.)

112. **Good troth,** in good truth.   Truly; the meaning also of 'good sooth'.

115. 'I thought you had better manners and more kindness at your command.'   Helena cannot understand the sudden transfer of Lysander's affections, and thinks he is making game of her.

117. **abused,** deceived, badly treated.

122. **heresies,** false doctrines.

124. **my surfeit and my heresy.**   Lysander means that he has had too much of Hermia, and that his former love for her was as mistaken as belief in a false doctrine.

126. **address,** direct, prepare.

132. **eat,** ate.

133. **prey,** preying or feeding.   (Fr. *proie*, Lat. *praeda*, booty.)

136. **an if,** if.

137. **of all loves,** by everything that is dear or loving, I beseech you to speak.

Act III—Scene 1

2. **Pat,** exactly, just.   (Cf. 'He had my name as pat as possible'.)

3. **rehearsal,** recital of a piece previous to public performance. Literally, to harrow again.   (*Re*, again, and O.F. *herse*, a harrow.)

4. **tiring-house,** attiring-house, where the actors changed their attire; 'dressing-room', we should say now.

7. **bully,** in Shakespeare's time a term of familiarity among boon companions, denoting a rough, good-tempered fellow.   The derivation of it is uncertain.   It may be a corruption of *burly*, or of the Ger. *Buhle*, a lover, or the Ital. *bullo*, a swaggering fellow.

8. **comedy,** a light humorous play.   (Either Gr. *komos*, a revel, or Gr. *kome*, a village, and *aeido*, I sing.)   Another instance of Bottom's ignorance.   No character in a comedy would " draw a sword to kill himself ".

12. **By 'r lakin,** by our ladykin or little lady, *i.e.* the Virgin Mary.

parlous, a corruption or contraction of 'perilous'.

15. **Not a whit,** not a little bit (O.E. *wiht*, anything.)   *Not* itself is a contraction of 'no whit'.

16. **prologue,** something spoken before.   (Gr. *pro*, before, *logos*, a speech.)

16, 17. **seem to say,** say in effect.

18. **more better,** emphatic comparative, common in Shakespeare's time.

22. **in eight and six,** in alternate lines of eight and six syllables. Called common metre, because many of the ballads and psalms were written in it.   (Cf. Sternhold and Hopkins' 1st psalm.)

24. **eight and eight**, each line containing eight syllables. (Cf. 100th Psalm.) "Eight and six" are not enough for Bottom.

25. **afeard**, a provincialism for 'afraid'; still used.

27. **to consider with yourselves**; a reflexive verb (like the Ger. *sich besinnen*, to ponder upon).

37. **defect**, for 'effect'; another of Bottom's blunders.

41. **pity of my life**, pity for my life, *i.e.* a sad thing for my life.

49. **calendar**, a register of the months. (Lat. *calendæ*, the first day of the Roman months.)

    almanac; from the Arabic *al*, the, and *manakh*, counting.

52. **casement**, the *case* or framework of a window. Then the window itself.

56. **lanthorn**. So written because the sides were originally made of horn. (The proper spelling is 'lantern', from Lat. *lanterna*.)

56, 57. **to disfigure or to present**, to figure or represent: more blunders.

65. **rough-cast**, plaster mixed roughly with small stones or grit.

66. **cranny**, chink. (Fr. *cran*; Ger. *Krinna*, a rent, a cleft.)

69. **every mother's son.** (See i. 2. 76.)

72. **cue**, the signal word, in acting, for the next speaker to begin. (According to some authorities, the letter Q was written at the end of a speech for *quando*, 'when', *i.e.* when the next actor was to begin. Or it may be from the Fr. *queue*, Lat. *cauda*, a tail, or ending.)

73. **hempen home-spuns**, rough fellows. A reference to garments made or spun at home from hemp, which would be of coarse material, and clumsily made.

75. **a play toward**, a play going on, or ready to go on.

84. He will be a stranger Pyramus than ever acted before, because Puck will play a trick upon him before he comes on again.

89–93. These lines are purposely nonsensical. Pyramus is at once lily-white and rose-red. Shakespeare was ridiculing the absurd literary attempts of country bumpkins.

91. **brisky juvenal**, brisk juvenile or youth.

    eke, also.

    Jew, simply because of '*ju*venal', and as a rime to 'hue'.

94. **Ninus**, the first King of Babylon. His tomb, which was a vast building, was at some distance from the city.

99. Bottom should have said: 'If I were, fair Thisby', *i.e.* If I were as true, &c. But he is intended to blunder; the blunder is all the more amusing because he knows nothing of his transformation.

102. **about a round**, a good way round about.

106, 107. Notice that all the verbs are placed in the first line, and the nouns belonging to them in corresponding order, in the second.

112, 113. **you see an ass-head of your own, do you?** This was a common expression in those days. Bottom of course was wholly ignorant of the fact that he was wearing an ass-head.

115. **translated,** transformed.

121. **ousel-cock,** the cock blackbird. Here the common blackbird is meant. The ring ousel is a larger species, with a white crescent on its breast.

123. **throstle,** thrush.

124. **little quill,** shrill or weak note.

127. ' The gray cuckoo with a plain or simple song.' The cuckoo never varies its note.

130. ' Who would enter into a contest of wit with so foolish a bird?'

131. **give the lie,** charge with falsehood.

136. **thy fair virtue's force,** the power of thy beauty.

139. He means that reason and love seldom go together: that many people love without reason, or contrary to reason.

142. **gleek,** jeer or jest. Bottom has been moralizing. He now says he can joke as well as be serious.

148. **whether.** Pronounce *where*.

150. **still,** always, constantly.

154. **pressed flowers,** that is, flowers which are pressed by you.

155, 156. ' I will purify the coarseness which thou, as a mortal, hast, so that thou shalt go light and airy as a spirit.'

157. **Cobweb,** a spider's web. (Flemish *kop*, a spider.)

160. **in his eyes,** *i.e.* in full view of him.

161. **apricocks,** apricots. (In Latin it was called *praecocia*, or early ripe. The Greek name was *praikokia*, which became in Arabic *barquq*, and, with the article *al*, *albarquq*. The Spaniards from this called it *albarcoque*, the French *abricot*, and the English *apricock*, and afterwards *apricot*.)

   dewberries, a species of blackberry which ripens before the common kind.

163. **humble-bee;** so called from its humming noise. It is also called ' bumble '-bee from the Latin *bombus*, a hum.

164-166. ' Gather the wax from the thighs of the bees, to make wax tapers of. Light these at the fiery eyes of the glow-worm, in order to light my love when going to bed and when rising.' The glow-worm's light is not in its eyes, but in its tail. Shakespeare probably used the eyes as being more poetical than the tail.

170. **Hail,** from the Low German *anhalen*, to call to.

174. ' I heartily beg your honours' pardon.'

178. **if I cut my finger.** It is a common practice still to put cobwebs over cuts, to stop the bleeding.

181. **Squash,** an unripe peascod or pea-pod.

186. **your patience;** perhaps used here in the same way as ' your honour ', &c., to denote one having patience or endurance. Or Bottom may mean that he is acquainted with the patience of Mustardseed.

195. **enforced,** outraged.

Act III—Scene 2

3. Which she must love with the greatest ardour.

5. **night-rule**, a corruption of 'night-revel', which was sometimes written 'night reuel'.

7. **close**, secret, private.

9. **A crew of patches**, a company of clowns. (Cf. Ger. *Tolpatsch*, a booby.)

　　rude mechanicals, rough mechanics.

10. In Shakespeare's time, the shops were open to the street, and in some cases 'stalls' projected from them, upon which such workmen as cobblers performed their work.

13. 'The most brainless booby of that stupid company.'

14. **presented**, represented.

15. **brake**, thicket.

17. **nole**, head. A similar word to *noddle*. (O.E. *knoll*, the top of anything.)

19. **mimic**, an actor, lit. one who imitates. (Lat. *mimicus*, cf. 'panto*mime*'.)

20. **the creeping fowler eye**, catch sight of the creeping fowler.

21. **Russet-pated choughs**, gray-headed jackdaws.

　　in sort, in company.

23. **Sever themselves**, separate.

24. **at his sight**, at sight of him.

25. **at our stamp**, at the sound of our footfall.

26. **He**, another.

27. 'The little sense they had they lost through their great fear, so that lifeless things began to injure them.'

30. All things catch something from them and they are too frightened to resist; some (things catch) sleeves; some (things catch) hats.

32. **translated**, transformed.

36. **latch'd**, smeared, anointed (Fr. *lécher*); or 'treated', as by a physician (O.E. *lacnian*, to cure); or 'moistened' (O.E. *leccan*, to water).

40. **That**, so that.

　　of force, perforce, of necessity.

41. **Stand close**, stand still. Keep quiet. To keep a thing 'close' is to keep it quiet.

44. **Lay breath on**, apply words to.

45. **but chide**, only chide or scold. (O.E. *chidan*, to scold.)

48. **o'er shoes in blood**. She means, 'having gone so far, now go a little farther'.

　　in, into.

53. **whole earth**, solid earth.

54, 55. 'The moon may creep through the centre of the earth, and give offence to the noonday—which the sun (her brother) is supplying to the people on the other side of the world—by appearing at the wrong time.'

57. **so dead,** so deathlike or pallid.

61. **Venus,** the planet.

62. 'What has this to do with my Lysander?'

68. **O, once tell true,** O, tell the truth for once.

70. **O brave touch!** O, brave deed!—ironical.

71. **a worm,** a snake.

72. **doubler tongue,** a more forked or cloven tongue. Adders do not sting with their tongues, but with their teeth.

74. 'You expend your passion in a mistaken caprice.' (O.F. *mesprendre,* to mistake.)

78. **therefor,** for it, thereby.

80. **so,** with this decision.

81. **whether.** Pronounce *where.*

82. **vein,** mood.

84–87. The weight of sorrow becomes still heavier when sleep refuses to pay what it owes, *i.e.* to come and cause forgetfulness. But if I stay here and wait for what he offers, he will pay me a little, *i.e.* I shall sleep a little.

90, 91. 'It must of necessity happen from thy mistake that some true love will be made false, not a false love be made true.'

92, 93. 'Then it is fate which ordains that for one who is true, there are a million who break oath after oath.'

95. **look thou find,** see that thou find.

96. 'She is quite sick with love, and pale in countenance.'

97. **that costs the fresh blood dear.** There was a belief in Shakespeare's time that every sigh cost the person sighing a drop of blood. *Costs* agrees with *love,* which is nearer to it than the real nominative "sighs".

99. **against,** by the time that.

101. **Tartar's bow.** The Tartars were famous for their skill in archery.

103. **Cupid's archery.** See act ii. 1. 157-9.

113. **lover's fee,** lover's payment or reward — which was three kisses.

114. **fond pageant,** the foolish show, or exhibition, they make of themselves. *Pageant* (L. Lat. *pagina*) first meant the platform on which the spectacle was shown, then the spectacle itself.

119. That must of necessity furnish sport beyond everything else.

121. **befall preposterously,** happen perversely.

122. Helena still thinks that Lysander and Demetrius are making game of her, and in this belief Hermia for a time shares.

124, 125. 'When vows are so born, all truth appears in them at their birth.'

127. **badge**, a distinguishing mark, generally the crest of a family. Lysander's badge consisted of his tears.

129. If what he is vowing to Helena be true, the professions he formerly made to Hermia must be false. That truth should contend with truth is both good and bad (devilish holy), because one truth wins, and the other is beaten.

131. 'You will ascertain the weight of nothing, because the two oaths will counterbalance each other, and both will prove as light as (idle) tales.'

135. **Nor none.** Note the emphatic double negative.

139. **Crystal is muddy**, *i.e.* compared with your eyes.

141. **Taurus**, a mountain range in Asia Minor.

144. **This princess of pure white**, this perfection of pure whiteness, *i.e.* her hand, which, if she gave it him, would be the seal or pledge of his happiness.

146. **To set against**, to set upon or attack.

150. **join in souls**, unite heartily.

153. **superpraise my parts**, overpraise my qualities. (Lat. *super*, above, over.)

157. **A trim exploit**, a pretty performance! (said in irony).

159. **sort**, kind, rank.

160, 161. **extort A poor soul's patience**, wring all the patience out of her, and so make her angry.

166. **bequeath**, *i.e.* do you bequeath.

169. **I will none**, *i.e.* of her; 'I do not want her'.

171. 'My heart stayed with her only after the manner of a guest.'

175. **thou aby it dear**, thou pay dearly for it. (*Aby* from O.E. *abiegan*, to redeem.)

177. **function**, office, duty, employment. (Lat. *fungor, functus*, to perform.)

179, 180. 'Night, while destroying the power of the eyes, makes the hearing doubly quick.'

182. **thy sound**, the sound of thee.

186. **bide**, abide or stay.

187. **engilds**, brightens.

188. **fiery oes**, fiery circles, orbs, *i.e.* the stars. O was frequently used for anything resembling a circle. There may be some pun intended on O's and I's.

189. **this**. 'Your love for me induces you to follow me, and so my hatred for you makes me leave you.'

194. 'To make this wicked sport in order to spite me.'

195. **Injurious**, insulting.

196, 197. **contrived To bait**, plotted to worry. (Cf. bear-baiting and bull-baiting.)

203. **artificial gods**, skilful gods. (The word usually means 'made by arts' rather than 'making by art' as here: Lat. *artificium*; *ars*, art; *facio*, I make.) Helena compares herself and Hermia to 'gods' simply in their capacity as 'creators'.

204. **neelds**, needles. (O.E. *nelde*.)

205. **sampler**, a piece of canvas on which *samples* or specimens of letters, figures, &c., were worked in wool. The working of samplers was a favourite means of spending leisure with ladies until quite recent years.

206. The *of* is not required, since 'warbling' is here a participle, not a verbal noun.

208. **incorporate**, incorporated, *i.e.* made one body. (Lat. *in*, into; and *corpus*, a body.)

209. **seeming**, seemingly.

210. **an union in partition**, something united though parted.

212-214. 'Outwardly we had two bodies, but inwardly one heart; two bodies crowned by one heart, as the two coats or blazons in heraldry (which belong to man and wife as one person) are crowned by one crest.' Heraldic language avoids referring to an object more than once by name. So here Shakespeare refers to "bodies" as "the first", as we would say "the former".

215. **rent**, an old form of *rend*.

220. **passionate**, in two syllables.

232. **so in grace**, so much in favour.

234. 'But most miserable, because I love, and am not loved in return.'

237. **persever** = persevere, keep on. Accent on second syllable.
   sad, grave, serious.

238. **Make mouths upon me**, make faces at me in derision.

239. **hold the sweet jest up**, keep up the delightful joke.

240. **well carried**, well carried on or managed.

242. **argument**, subject (of such a joke).

247. Hermia also thinks that Lysander is joking.

248. **entreat**, *i.e.* prevail by entreaty.

252. **that**, *i.e.* my life.

255. **withdraw**, come away.

257. **you Ethiope**, another allusion to Hermia's dark complexion.

257-259. We can only guess at the meaning of these lines. Demetrius probably begins by addressing Hermia: 'No, no, he'll do nothing rash'. Then he addresses Lysander in derision: 'Seem to break away from her, pretend to follow, but take care not to come. You are a cowardly fellow. Be off with you.'

260. **burr**, the head of the burdock plant, which clings to what it touches.

263. **tawny Tartar,** another jeer at Hermia's complexion. 'Tawny' is a corruption of *tanny*, the colour produced by tan.

267, 268. 'I wish I had your pledge that you would keep your word with me, for I perceive a weak tie keeps you back.' Hermia is still holding Lysander.

271. Hermia now perceives that the change in Lysander is real.

272. **what news, my love?** This is most probably a misprint for 'what means my love?'

274. **erewhile,** a little while before. *Ere*, before. (O.E. *aer*.)

279. **be out of,** be without.

280. 'Be sure nothing is truer.'

282. **juggler.** Pronounce as if three syllables.

canker-blossom, blossom-cankerer. Hermia means that Helena, like a canker-worm, has come by night and destroyed Lysander's love for her (Hermia).

286. **No touch of bashfulness,** no bashfulness, not even in the least degree.

290. **compare,** comparison.

291. **urged,** boasted of, asserted.

292. **personage,** figure.

295. **low,** short.

296. **maypole,** a pole erected on May-day to dance round. A common term of contempt applied to a tall woman.

300. **curst,** spiteful, ill-tempered.

302. **right maid,** a true maid as far as cowardice is concerned.

304. **something,** somewhat.

307. **evermore,** always.

310. **stealth,** stealing away.

314. 'And now, provided that you will let me go quietly.'

317. **simple and fond,** silly, and foolishly loving.

323. **shrewd,** sharp and spiteful with the tongue. (O.E. *schrewe*, malicious.)

324. **vixen,** an ill-tempered, spiteful girl or woman. Literally a she-fox. In the south 'fox' is still frequently pronounced 'vox'; *-en* is the O.E. feminine termination. This is the only word in which it survives. (Ger. *Füchsin*, a she-fox.)

329. **You minimus,** you very little creature. (Superlative of Lat. *parvus*, small.)

knot-grass. A kind of grass so called from the *knots* or joints of its stem. It was supposed to have the power of hindering the growth of children.

330. **You bead, you acorn,** both small articles, and generally of a dark colour, so that reference is made to Hermia's complexion as well as to her size.

331. 'On behalf of her who scorns your services.'

333. **intend**, pretend, exhibit.

335. **aby it**, atone for it, suffer for it.

335-337. 'Now she (Hermia) is not holding me, now follow if you dare, and let us prove by trial who has the greater right to Helena, you or I.'

338. **cheek by jole**, side by side, close together, cheek to jaw. (O.E. *ceole*, a jaw; now written 'jowl'.)

339. 'You, mistress, all this disturbance is owing to you.' 'All along of you' is still a common south-country expression.

340. **I.** Repeated here for emphasis. This is very common in French.

341. **curst**, mischievous, spiteful.

344. **amaz'd**, confused, bewildered.

345. **still**, always, constantly.

347. **shadows**, spirits.

352. **sort**, turn out, result.

353. **jangling**, quarrelling.

355. **Hie**, hasten so as to pant. (O.E. *higan*, to pant.)

356. **welkin**, sky. Properly the clouds. (Ger. *Wolken*, clouds.) Fairies were supposed to have the power of influencing the weather.

357. **Acheron.** In classical mythology, one of the four rivers of Hades or Hell. It was deep and black.

359. 'So that one may not come in the other's way.'

361. **wrong**, insult.

365. **batty wings**, bat-like wings, dark.

367. 'The juice of which has this beneficial quality.'

369. **wonted**, accustomed.

370, 371. **Derision** and **vision**, to be pronounced as four and three syllables respectively.

372. **wend**, turn. (Ger. *wenden*, to turn.) To go, with the idea of walking slowly.

373. **league**, *i.e.* bond of agreement. He means the marriage bond.

  date, duration.

379. **dragons**, fabulous winged monsters. In the classical mythology Night was drawn by horses. Ceres was the only goddess who had a team of dragons.

380. **Aurora**, the goddess of the dawn. Her 'harbinger' or forerunner is the morning star.

381. Ghosts always went home to the churchyards at the approach of dawn.

383. Executed criminals and suicides were buried formerly at crossroads. It was believed that the spirits of these, and of persons who

had been drowned, wandered about for one hundred years—as their bodies had not been properly buried.

386. **exile**, accent on second syllable.

387. **for aye**, constantly, always, ever. (O.E. *ava*, Ger. *je*, ever.)

389. **morning's love**, Cephalus, a man beloved by Aurora. He was fond of hunting, in which Oberon frequently joined him on the mountains near Athens.

391. **eastern gate**, whence the sun issued in the morning.

392. **Neptune**, the god of the sea. Here the sea itself.

402. **drawn**, with my sword drawn.

403. **straight**, straightway, at once.

404. **plainer**, more even, level.

413. **dares me on**, dares me to come on.

415. **lighter-heel'd**, swifter of foot.

418. **rest me**, rest myself.

420. **spite**, what he has done to spite me, injury.

422. **Abide**, wait for. ' Bide ' is still used in country places in the sense of to wait or stay. ' Bide here ' = ' stay here '.

I wot, I know. (O.E. *witan*, Ger. *wissen*, to know.)

426. **buy this dear**, pay dearly for this.

429. **To measure out my length**, to lie down at full length.

430. **look**, expect.

432. **Abate**, shorten.

Shine comforts, may comforts shine; subjunctive. So *steal* in line 436.

433. **back**, get back.

461–462. Proverbial expressions for ' Everything shall come right in the end '.

Act IV—Scene 1

2. **amiable**, beautiful, lovable.

coy, caress. (From the French *coi*; Lat. *quietus*, quiet; to caress, with the idea of making calm or quiet.)

8. **Mounsieur**, Bottom's rendering of ' Monsieur '.

11. **red-hipped**. One species of humble-bee has the upper part of the leg red.

13. **honey-bag**, the first stomach of the humble-bee, where it stows its honey. Country boys often kill the insect for the sake of its honey-bag.

16. **overflown with**, overflowed by.

19. **neaf**, fist. Spelt also *neif*. (Dan. *naeve*, O.E. *neve*, a list.)

20. **leave your courtesy**, leave off bowing.

22. **Cavalery**, Bottom's rendering of 'cavallero', the Spanish word corresponding with the French *cavalier* or *chevalier*, a horseman or knight, from the Latin *caballus*, a horse.

This should be Cavallero Pease-blossom, because Cobweb had been sent off for a honey-bag.

25. **tender ass.** Remember that Bottom is still unconscious of his appearance.

29. Music was perhaps obtained from the 'tongs' by striking them with a key, and the 'bones' were worked as they are now by nigger-minstrels (cf. the butchers' marrow-bones and cleavers). But the tongs may simply have been clashed like cymbals.

32. **Methinks**, it seems to me.

33. **bottle of hay**, a bundle or truss of hay. (O.F. *botel*, a small bundle.)

34. **fellow**, equal.

39. **exposition.** He means 'disposition'.

41. **be all ways away**, go away in all directions.

42. **Woodbine**, which elsewhere in Shakespeare means honeysuckle, is here generally supposed to be the convolvulus, which winds around the honeysuckle.

43. **female ivy**: because it clings to the elm as if married to it.

51. **rounded**, surrounded, encircled.

54. **orient**, from the east. (Lat. *oriens, orientis*, rising, *i.e.* sun-rising; afterwards applied to anything shining.)

58. **patience.** Pronounce in three syllables.

60. **her fairy**, the fairy in attendance.

61. **bower.** Pronounce in one syllable. The word bower was more commonly used for the ladies' apartment. (O.E. *búr*, a chamber.)

66. **the other**, the others.

67. **May all**, they may all.

69. **fierce**, confused.

73. **Dian's bud**, supposed to be the bud of the Agnus Castus or chaste tree. **Cupid's flower** was the heart's-ease.

81, 82. 'Strike the intelligence (or power of feeling) of all five of these more dead than ordinary sleep does.'

The five are Hermia, Helena, Lysander, Demetrius, and Bottom.

83. **charmeth sleep**, produces sleep as by a charm.

86. **rock the ground**, as a cradle.

87. **are new in amity**, have just made friends again. (Fr. *amitié*, friendship.)

88. **solemnly**, in ceremonious dance.

104. **our observation**, our observance of the morn of May. Cf. i. 1. 167.

105. **vaward of the day**, the early part of the day. 'Vaward' is a contraction of *avantwarde* or *avantgarde*. (*Warde*, O.F. for *garde*.)

108. **Dispatch.** The better spelling would be 'despatch'. (Fr. *dépêcher*, make haste.)

109-111. 'We will go to the top of the mountain, and notice the pleasing effect produced by the dogs' barking, and the echo of it.'

112. **Hercules.** See note on i. 2. 28.

Cadmus, a Phœnician king who came into Greece 1493 B.C. He built Thebes and introduced the use of letters into Greece. It is a mistake, chronologically, to bring Cadmus, Hercules, and Hippolyta together.

113. **Crete**, Candia, an island of the Mediterranean.

bay'd. 'To bay' means 'to bark at', from O.F. *abbayer*, to bark at. 'To bring to bay' means to drive the animal pursued to turn on his pursuers.

114. **Sparta**, the southern part of Greece. Its hounds were celebrated.

115. **chiding**, noise, barking.

120. **So flew'd**, having the same flews, or large overhanging lips.

so sanded, of the same sandy colour.

122. **dew-lapp'd.** See ii. 1. 50.

Thessaly, the northern part of Greece, famous for its bulls.

123. **match'd in mouth**, matched in sound, like a peal of bells. In forming a pack of hounds, care was taken to select dogs with graduated voices, so that their 'cry' should be harmonious.

124. **Each under each**, one lower-toned than the other.

cry, the sound made by hounds. Used also for the pack itself.

125. **holla.** Here it should be *halloa*, to call to. *Holla* means 'stop'.

126. **Crete, Sparta, Thessaly**, were all famous for their dogs.

127. **nymphs**, maidens. In classical mythology nymphs were demi-goddesses.

131. **I wonder of**, I wonder at.

134. **in grace of**, in honour of.

136. **answer of her choice**, answer concerning her choice (see i. 1. 83-90).

139. **Saint Valentine.** St. Valentine's day, 14th February, the day on which birds were supposed to select their mates.

147. **amazedly**, confusedly.

153. **Without the peril of**, beyond the reach of, or out of the danger threatened by.

154. **you have enough**, *i.e.* evidence to convict him on.

157. **defeated**, defrauded.

160. **stealth**, stealing away.

163. **in fancy**, for love.

164. **I wot**, I know. (O.E. *witan*, Ger. *wissen*, to know.)

179. **Overbear,** overrule.

187. **These things,** what has happened since the evening before.

191, 192. 'Just as a jewel does not belong to the person who finds it, but may be claimed by somebody else.'

206. **go about to,** try to.   Bottom is reluctant to own, even to himself, that he has passed the night as an ass.

209. **a patched fool,** a fool with a patched, or parti-coloured dress, *i.e.* motley.

210-213. Bottom's dazed condition is responsible for this jumble.

215. In Shakespeare's time a theatrical performance often concluded with songs and dances.

217, 218. **at her death,** at Thisbe's death—when, of course, it would be absurdly out of place.

Act IV—Scene 2

4. **transported,** transformed; or perhaps removed from this world by death, or by the fairies.

5, 6. **it goes not forward,** it will not be acted.

12. **paragon,** something supremely excellent.   (Spanish compound preposition *para*, *con*, in comparison, with.)

15, 16. 'If our play had proceeded, our fortunes would have been made.'

17, 18. **sixpence a day.**   This passage is supposed to have been a hint to Elizabeth to be more liberal to the stage.   She once bestowed twenty pounds a year upon a man whose acting pleased her.

21. **in Pyramus,** in the character of Pyramus.

23. **these hearts,** these dear fellows.   (Cf. the French expression *ce bon cœur*, and the sailor's 'my hearty'.)

24. **courageous,** glorious.

28. **right as it fell out,** exactly as it happened.

32. **good strings,** to tie your false beards on with.

33. **pumps,** shoes worn on special occasions, for *pomp* or ornament. The word is still used.

35. **preferred,** offered or presented to the authorities for approval. Bottom assumes that it will be accepted.

Act V—Scene 1

1. **that,** that which, what.

2. **may,** can, am able.

3. **antique**; accent the first syllable.   The meaning here is 'odd', not 'old'.

fairy toys, fanciful tales.

4. **seething brains**, brains always excited or agitated; lit ' boiling '.

5. **shaping fantasies**, creative imaginations.

apprehend, shape, construct.

8. **all compact**, entirely composed.

10. **all as frantic**, quite as frantic.

11. **Helen's beauty.** Helen was the wife of Menelaus, King of Sparta, and the most beautiful woman in the world.

brow of Egypt, a dark-complexioned face, like that of a gipsy. The gipsies were supposed to be Egyptians, of which their name is a corruption. They are still called ' Egyptians ' in some parts.

14. **bodies forth**, gives a bodily shape to.

21. **some fear**, some cause of fear.

23–27. ' But the account of the adventures of the night, and the fact that their minds have been so changed, prove that it is not all imagination; there is something consistent about it. Anyhow, it is certainly strange and wonderful.'

25. **More witnesseth**, bears testimony to more.

26. **constancy**, consistency.

27. **admirable**, wonderful. (Lat. *admirari*, to wonder at.)

30. **More**, more joy.

32. **masques**, entertainments in which the actors wore masks. They generally formed a part of wedding festivities. (Arabic, *maskharat*, a buffoon.) The word came to the English from the French *masque*.

34. **after-supper**, the rear-supper, corresponding to the modern dessert—or ' coffee '.

35. **manager of mirth**, master of the revels.

39. **abridgement**, an entertainment to abridge the time, *i.e.* to make it pass more quickly.

41. **The lazy time**, the slowly-moving time.

42. **a brief**, a statement, a list.

ripe, ready.

44. **the Centaurs**, in classical mythology, a race of beings living in Thessaly, half-man, half-horse. They attacked Hercules when he was pursuing the Erymanthian boar, but were routed by him.

47. **my kinsman.** Hercules and Theseus were distant cousins.

48. **Bacchanals**, people who took part in the revels in honour of Bacchus the wine-god, during which they drank as much wine as they could.

49. **the Thracian singer**, Orpheus, the famous musician of Thrace. He was so grieved at the death of his wife Eurydice, that he treated with contempt the tipsy Bacchanals (some Thracian women), who in revenge tore him to pieces.

50. **device**, performance.

52, 53. If Shakespeare alluded to any actual event in these two lines, it was probably the death of Robert Greene the dramatist, which took place in 1592, in extreme poverty. Greene was Master of Arts of both universities (Oxford and Cambridge), and always so styled himself on the title-page of his works.

52. **thrice three muses,** the nine goddesses who, in Greek mythology, presided over the arts, &c.

55. **Not sorting with,** not suitable to.

59. Pronounce **wondrous** as *wondĕrous*.

strange snow. Here we expect something strongly in contrast with snow, as ' hot ' is in contrast with ' ice '. We must take *strange snow* to mean snow which is the reverse of all other snow.

60. **concord of this discord,** the agreement of this apparent opposition in terms. In music every chord technically known as a ' discord ' must be ' resolved' on or followed by a ' concord '. Shakespeare may have had this in mind.

65. **fitted,** suited to his part.

68. **Which** is made to do duty both as the object of ' rehearsed' and the subject of ' made '.

70. **passion,** emotion.

74, 75. 'And have now exercised their untrained memories with this play in preparation for your nuptials.'

77. **It is not for you.** It is not a play fit for you.

79, 80. ' Unless you can find sport in their endeavours, which they have strained to the utmost, in order to learn the parts, which they have studied with cruel pain.'

80. **conn'd,** studied.

83. **simpleness,** simplicity, single-heartedness.

85. **o'ercharged,** loaded beyond what it can bear.

88. **in this kind,** of this nature: *i.e.* of the nature of a play. Theseus plays on the word in *kinder.*

91, 92. ' Noble consideration accepts the effort to please, without regarding the merit of the performance.'

93. **great clerks,** great scholars.

95. **Where,** when.

96. **Make periods,** make full stops.

97. **Throttle,** choke. (O.E. *throte,* Ger. *Drossel,* the throat.)

101. **fearful,** full of fear, timid.

105. ' The less they say, the more they express, as far as I am able to understand.'

106. **address'd,** prepared, ready.

Flourish of trumpets. In Shakespeare's time this served the purpose of the modern ' overture ' by the band.

113. **minding,** intending

118. 'This fellow does not pay any attention to his stops. In Quince's prologue the stops are all in the wrong places, so that he generally says exactly the opposite of what he means.

120. **the stop,** a term in horsemanship—of course a quibble on the other meaning.

123. **recorder,** a flute with a mouthpiece like a flageolet

in government, *i.e.* he produces the notes, but not in the proper order; they are not under control.

129. **certain,** certainly.

130. **present,** represent.

134–136. The legends of the man in the moon were invented to account for the spots on the moon's surface. They are three in number. One says the man is Isaac carrying a bundle of sticks for the sacrifice of himself. Another, that he is Cain; and a third asserts that he is the Israelite who is described in the Book of Numbers as having gathered sticks on the Sabbath day.

138. **grisly,** terrible. (O.E. *gryslic,* Ger. *grässlich,* terrible.)

hight, is called. (Ger. *heisst,* is called.)

141. **fall,** let fall.

145, 146. These lines are in ridicule of the alliteration of which the small poets of Shakespeare's time were so fond. Shakespeare ridiculed it also in *Love's Labour's Lost.*

146. **broach'd,** stabbed. Literally *spitted.* (Fr. *broche,* a spit.)

162. **sinister,** left. (Latin.) Accent on second syllable.

180. **sensible,** sentient, capable of feeling.

194. **Limander.** He means Leander, the youth of Abydos, who used to swim across the Hellespont every night to Sestos to visit Hero (not Helen). One stormy night he was drowned, and Hero in despair threw herself into the sea.

196. **Shafalus to Procrus.** He means Cephalus to Procris. Cephalus was beloved by Aurora, but he remained true to his wife Procris.

200. **Ninny,** Ninus.

201. **'Tide life, 'tide death,** whether life or death betide, or befall me.

204. **mural,** wall. (Lat. *murus,* a wall.)

206, 207. 'When walls are so perverse as to hear people's secrets, there is nothing to be done but to pull them down.'

209, 210. 'The best actors are but shadows of the reality; the worst may be made equal to them by the aid of imagination.'

221. **A lion.** Snug wishes to show the audience that he is no lion. Therefore some commentators write 'No lion'. Another writes 'lion-fell', meaning, a lion's skin. Others suggest that 'nor meaning *neither* may be understood before 'A lion fell'. **fell,** cruel.

dam, a mother. Applied to quadrupeds. (Fr. *dame,* Lat *domina.*)

223. 't were pity on my life. See note on iii. 1. 41.

237. He is no crescent, he is no crescent-shaped or new moon. When the half-moon stage is reached the horns are no longer to be seen.

244. for the candle, because of the candle.

245. in snuff. Demetrius puns here. The old-fashioned candles were said to be 'in snuff' when the charred wick deadened the light. 'In snuff' also meant to be offended.

246. would, I would, I wish.

249. in the wane, decreasing, like the moon towards the end of the month. Theseus means that he is coming to the end of his speech. (O.E. *wanian*, to grow wan, or faint.)

264. moused, treated as a mouse is by a cat; shaken and torn.

267. sunny; another ridiculous expression. So 'golden' in line 269.

269, 270. Observe the alliteration.

273. dole, grief. (Lat. *dolor*.)

279. ye Furies. The Furies were three in number, and executed the vengeance of the gods.

280. Fates. There were also three Fates in classical mythology, who controlled every man's destiny. Clotho, the youngest, presided over his birth, and held a distaff in her hand. Lachesis spun out all the events and actions of his life, and Atropos, the eldest, cut the thread when the web was complete, *i.e.* when his life ended.

281. thrum, the small tuft at the end of the thread, where it was fastened to the loom. 'To cut thread and thrum' means 'to cut everything'.

282. Quail and quell both mean the same thing, viz. to kill. (O.E. *cwellan*, to kill.)

283. passion, violent grief. Cf. line 70.

285. Beshrew my heart, lit. 'evil befall my heart'. (O.E. *schrewe*, wicked.) But it is simply an exclamation.

289. with cheer, with cheerfulness. Lit. 'with face', *i.e.* with a *pleasant* face. Cf. i. 1. 122.

290. confound; probably 'mingle as you fall'. But one can never be sure that Pyramus (*i.e.* Bottom) means anything.

292. pap, breast. (O. Swed. *papp*, the breast.)

302. No die, but an ace, no die except an ace. Demetrius makes a double pun here. *Die* is the singular of 'dice', and he pronounces 'ace' (the die marked with only one spot) 'ass'.

308. How chance, how does it chance, or happen, that.

311. passion; see line 283.

314. mote, the smallest possible thing. (O.E. *mot*, a mote.)

which Pyramus, &c., which is the better, Pyramus or Thisbe.

319. **means**, says, or goes on to say. (Ger. *Was meinen Sie?* what do you say?)

videlicet (generally written *viz.*), namely. (Lat. *licet*, it is allowed, you may, and *videre*, to see.)

331. **His eyes were green.** Green eyes used to be considered very beautiful.

332. **Sisters Three**, the Fates. See line 280.

336. **shore** for *shorn*, to suit the rime.

340. **imbrue**, stain with blood. (O.F. *embruer*.)

346, 347. **the wall is down that parted their fathers**; a proverbial expression for 'the cause of difference between them is removed'.

348. **Bergomask dance**, a country-dance. So called from Bergamo, a town of Lombardy, the inhabitants of which were considered clownish by the Venetians.

350. **epilogue**, something spoken after a play: generally an apology for the play and the acting of it. (Gr. *epilogus*, a concluding speech.)

357. **told**, counted. (O.E. *tellan*, to count: cf. "He *telleth* the number of the stars".)

358. **fairy time**, midnight.

360. **overwatch'd**, been up through, passed in wakefulness.

361. **palpable - gross**, so clumsy that everyone may perceive its roughness. (Lat. *palpare*, to feel.)

363. **A fortnight hold we**, *i.e.* let us keep up *for* a fortnight.

366. **behowls**, howls at.

368. **All**, *i.e.* utterly.

fordone, worn out, exhausted, quite done. *For*, like the German *ver*, has an intensive force.

369. **wasted brands**, fires or torches that have burnt low. See line 385.

370. **screech-owl.** The note of the screech-owl was supposed to be an omen of death.

378. **triple**, so called from her threefold sovereignty. She was called Luna, Cynthia, or Phœbe, in Heaven; Diana, on earth; and Hecate, in Hades or Hell. In this place she would be more correctly called by one of her first names.

team. Like Phœbus the sun-god, the moon-goddess drove round the sky in a chariot.

381. **frolic**, merry. (Ger. *fröhlich*, gay.)

384. **behind the door**, where it would not be seen. Puck was supposed to help good girls with their household work.

389. **this ditty**, a song. No words are here given. Probably the song was changed at different performances to suit the particular local circumstances. (O.F. *dite*, O.E. *ditee*, a kind of poem.)

390. **dance it,** here means simply 'dance'; cf. 'trip it'. The *it* is here used instead of the cognate accusative, *i.e.* an object of the same meaning as the verb; *e.g.* to dance a dance.

391. **your song.** Probably another song lost.

by rote, by heart.

401. **blots of Nature's hand,** such as are mentioned in line 403 which are caused by malignant fairies.

403. **hare-lip,** an upper lip with a cleft in it, as in a hare.

404. **prodigious,** unnatural.

405. **nativity,** birth.

407. **consecrate,** consecrated.

408. **take his gait,** take his way.

409. **several,** separate.

415. **shadows**; either spirits, or such shadows as Theseus mentioned in speaking of actors (see line 209).

416. **but this,** the clause in lines 417, 418.

424, 425. 'If we have the luck, which we do not deserve, to escape being hissed.'

429. **Give me your hands,** give me the sound of your hands, *i.e.* your applause.

APPENDIX

1. DATE OF THE PLAY

The first printed edition of *A Midsummer-Night's Dream* was issued in the year 1600 by Thomas Fisher, when it is mentioned as having been several times publicly acted. Another edition was published in the same year by James Roberts. But as this was done without authority, it was withdrawn by order of the lord chamberlain, of whose company of players Shakespeare was a member. It is important, however, as having been the basis from which the play was printed in the folio edition of 1623.

The play is generally supposed to have been written in honour of some nobleman's wedding—whose, we do not know. There is so very little evidence, either external or internal, to fix the date of its composition, that critics vary widely in their opinion on the point. Some place it as early as 1590; others as late as 1598. The correct date is probably between these two.

The only external evidence we have is derived from a little book called *Palladis Tamia or Wit's Treasury*, by Francis Meres, published in 1598. Here the play is mentioned in a list of Shakespeare's comedies, which proves that it must have been written and performed before that date. The internal evidence is vague, and only furnishes suppositions. If the death of Robert Greene is referred to in act v. 52, 53, as some critics suppose, we should have 1592 (in which year Greene died) as the earliest limit. Titania's account of the disastrous results of her quarrel with Oberon (see act ii. sc. 1) contains a description of a summer very like that of 1594, which was exceedingly wet and cold. This suggests the theory that the play was written and performed either at the end of 1594 or at the beginning of 1595, when the circumstances would be fresh in the poet's mind, and the allusions to them would be understood and appreciated by the audience.

But although we are not able to fix the exact date of the

composition of *A Midsummer-Night's Dream*, we are quite safe in putting it among Shakespeare's earlier plays. Like the early works of most writers of the time, it abounds in puns, conceits, and classical allusions, and the blank verse consists of unbroken and smoothly flowing lines. The boldness of expression, the seriousness and depth of thought which characterize the later plays, are altogether wanting here. Rime, which is generally indicative of early work, was undoubtedly essential, and would have been used at any period in dealing with such a subject. Adopting the views of the majority of critics, we may decide upon the period 1594–1596 as the most probable date, and classify the play as the last and best of a group which includes the *Comedy of Errors*, *Love's Labour's Lost*, *All's Well that Ends Well*, and *The Two Gentlemen of Verona*.

2. SOURCES OF THE PLOT AND CHARACTERS

The plot of *A Midsummer-Night's Dream* must be considered under four heads, viz. :

(1) The marriage of Theseus and Hippolyta.
(2) The rehearsal of the interlude by the Athenian mechanics, and its performance on the wedding night.
(3) The adventures of the lovers.
(4) The quarrel of Oberon and Titania, and their reconciliation through the agency of Puck, by whom also the difficulties of the lovers are satisfactorily arranged.

These four elements, although distinct, are intimately connected : (1) and (2), and (3) and (4) obviously so. The lovers and their relatives are attached to the court, and the decision as to the marriage of the former rests with Theseus. Oberon and Titania are friends of Theseus and Hippolyta, and are naturally interested in their wedding.

(1) *Theseus and Hippolyta.* — Shakespeare's knowledge of Theseus was derived from Sir Thomas North's translation of Plutarch's *Lives*. Here there are two accounts of the hero's marriage. According to one, the name of the Amazon whom he took prisoner and married was Antiope; according to the other it was Hippolyta. Chaucer in his *Knight's Tale* adopts the latter name, and Shakespeare no doubt followed his version.

(2) *The Interlude.*—The story of Pyramus and Thisbe is taken from Ovid's *Metamorphoses*. Shakespeare probably derived his knowledge of it from three sources:

(i) Golding's translation of the fifteen books of the *Metamorphoses*, which was published, in parts, at various times between 1564 and 1574.
(ii) Chaucer's *Tale of Thisbe of Babylon* (adapted from Ovid).
(iii) Clement Robinson's *A new Sonet* (short poem) *of Pyramus and Thisbe.*

From many expressions in this and other plays, Golding appears to have been Shakespeare's great authority on all subjects connected with the classical mythology. He was probably well acquainted with Chaucer's Tales also. Robinson's Sonet deals with the subject in the affected style known as Euphuism, from Euphues, the hero of a work by John Lyly. The conversation of Euphues and his friends is characterized by exaggerated vivacity, far-fetched conceits, and excessive alliteration. The imitators of Lyly carried his eccentricities to an absurd extent. It is the writers of this school whom Shakespeare ridicules in the high-flown speeches of the rustics in the interlude, notably in such lines as these:

> "Whereat, with blade, with bloody blameful blade,
> He bravely broach'd his boiling bloody breast".

The story of Pyramus and Thisbe was not only well known to Shakespeare, but it must have been a favourite theme of many a body of amateur performers, such as Bottom and his friends. Acting was a popular diversion of the country-folk in Elizabeth's time, and continued to be so in a constantly diminishing degree down to comparatively recent years. The Mummers, who delighted the children at Christmas time, are still well remembered in many country districts.

(3) *The Lovers.*—The episode of the lovers is, as far as we know, original. The mysterious effect produced upon them by the love-juice would not greatly surprise an audience of Shakespeare's time, when the belief in the magical properties of plants and flowers was very wide-spread.

(4) *The Fairies*, &c. — Shakespeare's fairy-lore has been described as "An attempt to blend the Elves of the village with the

Fays of romance". Like the former, his sprites are so small as to be invisible to mortals; they are fond of dancing in circles, and are given to child-stealing. Oberon with his train of knights, and Titania, the queen, with her court of fairies, belong to romance, and were brought prominently into notice in England by Spenser's *Faerie Queen*, published in 1590.

Oberon was originally the German fairy Alberich or Elferich, meaning Elf King, under which name he figured in much early German poetry. The French borrowed him and called him first Alberon, and then Auberon. In the French romance of Huon de Bordeaux, which deals with the affairs of Charlemagne and his peers, Auberon acts as the protector of the hero Huon. This romance was translated into English by Lord Berners in 1534, and the fairy-king is called Oberon, as he is by Spenser in the *Faerie Queen*. Lord Berners' book was exceedingly popular in London, and Shakespeare was probably well acquainted with it.

Titania.—The queen of the fairies is known by various names. Shakespeare himself calls her Queen Mab in *Romeo and Juliet*, and to Chaucer she is known as Proserpine. Titania is one of the names given to Diana in the classical mythology, and probably Shakespeare found it in Golding's Ovid. The nymphs who accompanied Diana in her hunting excursions would suggest the idea of the fairy queen's attendant sprites.

Puck, better known as Robin Goodfellow, was the genuine village-elf, and was believed in by country folk from time immemorial, as the author of most of the mischief and minor troubles of everyday life. He was good-natured to those who pleased him, and assisted them in such actions as churning, corn-grinding, sweeping, &c.

Puck was known in most of the northern countries of Europe, but rather as a generic than a proper name. In Icelandic he was called a *puki*, in Danish a *puk*, in Irish a *pooca*, and in Welsh a *pwcca*. All these variations of the same word mean an *elf* or *sprite*. Robin Goodfellow is perhaps the same as the German 'unser Knecht Ruprecht', and the term 'Hob-goblin' is a corruption of 'Rob-goblin'. The latter name pleased him, and those who applied it to him or called him 'sweet Puck' were pretty sure of his help. In his love of flattery Puck resembled other similar beings. The Irish found it prudent to call their fairies the good people' — the Scotch theirs 'the good neighbours', while those terrible beings the Furies were mentioned by the Greeks as the 'gracious goddesses'.

3. CRITICAL REMARKS

It has been before suggested that *A Midsummer - Night's Dream*—which is rather of the nature of a Masque or Interlude than a regular drama—was written for, and acted on, the occasion of some nobleman's wedding. Nor is this improbable, seeing that marriage festivities often included performances of this kind, and that Shakespeare numbered several noblemen among his patrons and friends. The subject of a Masque is allegorical or mythological, and is generally told in rime. It depends for its interest greatly on the scenery, the music, the songs, and the dancing. In *A Midsummer-Night's Dream* these four elements preponderate.

We might suppose from the name of the play that the action is laid on the night of the 24th of June, whereas all the dreams happened at the end of April and the beginning of May. But Midsummer's Day was a day of great rejoicing and frolic, which generally ended with plays of a light and fanciful character. The name, therefore, implied a play *suitable to be acted on Midsummer Night*, a time when, above all others, fairies, ghosts, witches, &c., were active. Shakespeare calls it a dream, because, as he plainly indicates, he wishes us to regard it almost entirely as a creation in which fancy and imagination pursue their way, uncontrolled by reason and probability—just as our thoughts do during sleep. The principal characters compare their experiences to a dream. Titania dreams that she is enamoured of an ass. Bottom considered his dream wonderful enough to be the subject of a ballad. The two pairs of lovers, after awaking from sleep, and holding conversation with the duke and his train, are for some time in doubt as to whether they are not still dreaming. Theseus regards their stories as nothing else than dreams and fancies, and the Epilogue begs the audience so to consider the play.

The drama of Shakespeare which bears the greatest resemblance to *A Midsummer - Night's Dream* is *The Tempest*. In both, the machinery is supernatural, but there is almost all the difference that we might expect to find between one of the earliest, and one of the latest, works of a great writer. In the early play the fairies are very small, and have superhuman power; but, on the other hand, they have all the weaknesses and evil passions of men. Oberon and Titania quarrel and wrangle, and are as jealous and spiteful as two human beings might be. But they are not creations of the poet's. Neither is Puck, and Shakespeare had to leave them in a measure as he found them, and as they existed in the popular imagination. Puck, although a refined Robin Goodfellow, has most of the failings of the sprite who delighted in mischief, and whose chief amusement was to cause vexation, and lead folks astray. In *The Tempest*, Prospero's agent Ariel is an airy spirit, an ethereal being, who is above human weaknesses, and whose sole, intense longing is for liberty. In *The Tempest*, man commands the spirits, whereas in *A Midsummer-Night's Dream* he is under their control.

There is little to be said about the human mortals in the play, because as characters in a dream they can have no strong individuality. So Lysander and Demetrius are very commonplace young men—and, excepting that Demetrius is more fickle-minded than Lysander, there is little to distinguish them but their names. Hermia and Helena certainly have different characteristics, the former being short and dark, the latter tall and fair. Hermia is pert and vixenish; Helena a meek and timid maiden, never bad-tempered, and always ready to give way. But they are feeble personages, and both they and Hippolyta are such as we might expect from the pen of an immature dramatist.

Theseus represents "Shakespeare's early ideal of an heroic warrior and man of action". He possesses great strength of mind, will, and body, with the kindness and consideration which the consciousness of such strength gives. His gentleness and courtesy in no way impair his authority, which is willingly submitted to by all.

But the chief interest of the play centres in the Athenian clowns, particularly in Bottom. This individual is perfectly good-tempered and thoroughly conceited, and his fellows have just as high an opinion of him as he has of himself. The nominal manager of their Interlude is Peter Quince, but he defers in everything to Bottom, who orders him and the others about as he pleases, without the least remonstrance on their part. Circumstances have no effect on Bottom's characteristics. During his 'translation' he is as conceited and dictatorial with the fairies and their queen as he is with his friends, and, during the performance of the Interlude, the duke learns by experience that he has at least one subject who is not afraid to contradict and correct him, in his own palace.

Nothing in the play is Greek, excepting the names. Theseus might be an English baron of the middle ages, returning from the wars, and settling down among his vassals and friends. The action is laid at Athens, but everything is English—scenery, customs, plants, and flowers, such as Shakespeare knew. Bottom and his friends are country mechanics, such as Shakespeare must have often seen acting at Easter and Christmas, and on other high days and holidays, of which there were many in the Merrie England of Elizabeth.

Highways and Byways of English Literature
BLACKIE'S ENGLISH TEXTS

Edited by W. H. D. ROUSE, Litt.D.

General Literature

ADDISON—**Essays from " The Spectator ".**
The Story of Sir Roger de Coverley.
Adventures on the Seas by English Sailors in the Great Days of Old.
ÆSOP—**Fables from Æsop.**
HANS ANDERSEN—**Fairy Tales.**
JANE AUSTEN—**Emma.**
BACON—**Essays.** 37 of the Essays.
ISABELLA BIRD — **A Lady's Life in the Rocky Mountains.**
BOCCACCIO—**Tales from the Decameron.**
BORROW—**Gipsy Stories.**
The Stories of Antonio and Benedict Mol.
BOSWELL—**Life of Johnson.**
BUNYAN—**Pilgrim's Progress.** Part I.
BURKE—**Speeches on America.**
CARLYLE—**The Hero as Divinity; Man of Letters.**
The Hero as Poet; as King.
CERVANTES — **Don Quixote** (abridged).
COBBETT—**Rural Rides.**
COWLEY—**Essays.**
DEFOE — **Captain Singleton's Early Adventures.**
Journal of the Plague Year.
Robinson Crusoe.
DELONEY—**Thomas of Reading and John Winchcombe.**
The Gentle Craft.
DE QUINCEY—**The English Mail Coach,** &c.
DICKENS—**A Christmas Carol.**
The Chimes.
The Cricket on the Hearth.
DICKENS & COLLINS — **The Wreck of the " Golden Mary ".**
MARIA EDGEWORTH—**Castle Rackrent.**
Election Scenes in Fiction.
GEORGE ELIOT—**The Mill on the Floss** (abridged).
ERASMUS—**The Praise of Folly.**
MRS. GASKELL—**Cranford.**
GATTY—**Parables from Nature.**
GOSSE—**The Romance of Natural History.**
GRIMM—**Fairy Tales.**
LADY CHARLOTTE GUEST—**Stories from The Mabinogion.**

NATHANIEL HAWTHORNE—**Tanglewood Tales.**
HAZLITT — **Characters from Shakespeare's Plays.**
HERBERT OF CHERBURY—**Life of Lord Herbert of Cherbury.** Autobiography.
HUGO—**The Toilers of the Sea.**
WASHINGTON IRVING—**England's Rural Life and Christmas Customs.**
Rip Van Winkle, &c.
KINGSLEY—**The Heroes.**
The Water-Babies.
LAMB—**Adventures of Ulysses.**
Tales from Shakspeare.
Schooldays and other Essays.
E. W. LANE—**Tales from the Arabian Nights.**
Sindbad the Sailor. From E. W. Lane's *Arabian Nights.*
LUCIAN—**Trips to Wonderland.**
MALORY—**Coming of Arthur.**
The Knights of the Round Table.
HERMAN MELVILLE — **Moby Dick: or, The Whale.**
MILTON—**Areopagitica,** &c.
MORE—**Utopia.**
MOTTE - FOUQUÉ — **Sintram and his Companions.**
PEPYS — **Passages from the Diary of Samuel Pepys.**
POE—**The Gold Bug,** &c.
ROPER—**The Life of Sir Thomas More.**
RUSKIN—**Byzantine Churches of Venice.**
Crown of Wild Olive.
Sesame and Lilies.
MICHAEL SCOTT — **Tom Cringle's Log.**
SIR WALTER SCOTT — **Wallace and Bruce.**
ANNA SEWELL—**Black Beauty.** Part I.
SMOLLETT—**Scenes from the Travels of Humphry Clinker.**
SWIFT—**Gulliver's Travels.**
THEOPHRASTUS—**Characters.**
WALPOLE — **Letters on the American War of Independence. Letters on France and the French Revolution.**
WALTON—**Complete Angler.**

BLACKIE'S ENGLISH TEXTS—*Contd.*

Travel

ANSON — The Taking of the Galleon. From *Lord Anson's Voyage Round the World* (1743).

BOSWELL—The Journal of a Tour to the Hebrides with Samuel Johnson, LL.D.

CAPTAIN COOK — Captain Cook's Second Voyage.

SIR FRANCIS DRAKE—The World Encompassed (1628).

LORD DUFFERIN — Letters from High Latitudes.

HAKLUYT — The French in Canada.

SIR RICHARD HAWKINS— Voyage into the South Sea.

EVARISTE RÉGIS HUC — A Sojourn at Lhassa. Travels in Thibet.

WASHINGTON IRVING — Companions of Columbus.

CAPTAIN JAMES—The Voyage of Captain James (1633).

MUNGO PARK—Travels in the Interior of Africa.

POLO — The Travels of Marco Polo.

SAMUEL PURCHAS — Roe's Embassy to the Great Mogul. Early Voyages to Japan (1625).

RALEIGH—The Discovery of Guiana.

SMITH, B. WEBSTER—Pioneers of Exploring.

History

BEDE—History of the Church of England. Down to A.D. 709.

ROBERT BLAKENEY—The Retreat to Corunna.

Britain and Germany in Roman Times.

BURKE—Speeches on America.

CLARENDON — Cavalier and Roundhead.

PHILIPPE DE COMMINES — Warwick the Kingmaker.

FROISSART—Border Warfare under Edward III and Richard II.

Reign of Richard II.
Crecy and Poitiers.

GIBBON—The Age of the Antonines.

HAKLUYT—The Spanish Armada, &c.

HOLINSHED—England in the Sixteenth Century.

RICHARD KNOLLES — Wars with the Turks.

LIVY—Hannibal in Italy.

MACAULAY—Macaulay's History. Chapter I. Before 1660. Chapter II. Under Charles II. Chapter III. England in 1685.
Essay on Clive.
Essay on Hastings.
Essay on Hampden.
Second Essay on Pitt, Earl of Chatham.
Essay on Sir William Temple.

AMMIANUS MARCELLINUS— Julian the Apostate.

MONTLUC—The Adventures of Montluc.

MOTLEY—William the Silent. Alva (1567-8).

NAPIER—Battles of the Peninsular War. 2 vols.
1. Coruña, Talavera, Badajos.
2. Salamanca, Siege of Burgos, Vittoria, Siege of San Sebastian.

LORD NELSON—The Battle of the Nile. Dispatches and Letters.

ORME—The Black Hole of Calcutta and the Battle of Plassey.

PLUTARCH—Life of Pompey.
Themistocles and Pericles.
Aristeides and Marcus Cato.
Alcibiades and Demosthenes.
Alexander. Julius Cæsar.
Brutus and Coriolanus.

PRESCOTT—Montezuma.
The Capture of Mexico.
The Conquest of Peru.

SCOTT—Wallace and Bruce.

JOHN SMITH—Early History of Virginia (1627).

THUCYDIDES—The Siege of Syracuse.

WALPOLE—Letters on the American War of Independence.
Letters on France and the French Revolution.

DUKE OF WELLINGTON— Waterloo. Dispatches of Wellington, &c.

BLACKIE'S
STANDARD ENGLISH CLASSICS

With Introductions and generally with Notes

Cloth boards. Price 2s. 6d. each

Life and Action. An Anthology of Prose. Selected and edited by W. H. J. Richardson.

English Lyrical Types. An Anthology. B. J. Pendlebury, M.A.

Readings in English Literature. From Chaucer to Dickens. B. G. Aston, B.A.(Oxon.). With Time-Chart and Biographical Notes.

Cloth boards. Price 2s. each

BACON—Essays.

CHAUCER—Canterbury Pilgrims. William Ferguson, M.A.

Eighteenth-Century Anthology, An. (No Notes.)

Elizabethan Poetry—A Pageant of Elizabethan Poetry.

EMERSON—Representative Men.

Epic Poetry—English Tales in Verse. C. H. Herford, Litt.D.

Essays—English Essays. John Lobban, M.A.

GOLDSMITH—She Stoops to Conquer and The Good-natured Man. H. Littledale, M.A., Litt.D. **The Citizen of the World.** Selected Letters. W. A. Brockington.

Historical Literature — English Historians. A. J. Grant, M.A.

HOLMES—Autocrat of the Breakfast-Table.

JOSEPHUS—Autobiography and Selections from the Jewish War.

KINGLAKE—Eothen.

Letters—Letters of Great Writers. Rev. Hedley V. Taylor, B.A., M.A.

Longer Poems of the Nineteenth Century. Edward Parker, M.A., Ph.D., Dip.Ed. First Series, 1800-50, 2s. Second Series, 1850-1900, 2s.

Longer Poems of To-day. Edward Parker.

Lyric Poetry—English Lyric Poetry. Frederic Ives Carpenter, M.A.

MACAULAY—Essay on Warren Hastings. Essay on Clive. Lives of Johnson and Goldsmith.

MARCUS AURELIUS—A Selection from the Meditations of Marcus Aurelius Antoninus.

Masques—English Masques. H. A. Evans, M.A.

MILTON—Paradise Lost. Books X, XI, and XII.

Pastorals—English Pastorals. E. K. Chambers, C.B., B.A., D.Litt.

PLUTARCH— Lives of Greek Heroes.

REYNOLDS (SIR JOSHUA)—Discourses on Art. A Selection.

Satires—English Satires. Oliphant Smeaton, M.A.

SCOTT—Anne of Geierstein. Ivanhoe. Kenilworth. Legend of Montrose. Old Mortality. Quentin Durward. Rob Roy. The Talisman.

Seventeenth-Century Anthology, A.

Sixteenth-Century Anthology, A.

SOUTHEY—Life of Nelson. David Frew, B.A.

SPENSER—The Faery Queene, I. The Faery Queene. Book II. The Faery Queene. Book V.

Cloth boards. Price 1s. 9d. each

BROWNING—Strafford.

BYRON—Childe Harold's Pilgrimage. Complete. **Childe Harold's Pilgrimage.** Cantos I and II.

DRYDEN—Essay of Dramatic Poesy.

KINGSLEY—The Heroes.

MACAULAY—England in 1685 (The Third Chapter of *Macaulay's History*).

MACAULAY—Essay on Addison. Essay on Horace Walpole. Essay on Milton. Essay on William Pitt, Earl of Chatham. (First Essay.) **Selections from Macaulay's Essays.** H. M. King, B.A.

MARLOWE—Edward the Second.

MILTON—Lycidas.

POPE—Essay on Criticism.

THACKERAY—The Rose and the Ring. J. G. Fyfe, M.A. (No Notes.)

P.T.O.

BLACKIE'S STANDARD ENGLISH CLASSICS—(Cont.)

Cloth boards. Price 1s. 6d. each

ADDISON—**Selected Essays from the Spectator.** Rev. Henry Evans.

AUSTEN—**Northanger Abbey.** R. F. Patterson, M.A., D.Litt.

BYRON—**Childe Harold's Pilgrimage.** Cantos III and IV. John Downie, M.A., and David Frew.

CARLYLE—**Essay on Burns.**

CHAUCER—**The Prologue to the Canterbury Tales.** E. F. Willoughby.

The Nonne Prest His Tale. R. F. Patterson, M.A., D.Litt.

DICKENS — **Short Stories from Dickens.** J. G. Fyfe, M.A. (No Notes.)

English Poetry—A Book of Comparative Poetry. Being Typical Poems arranged for Comparative Study. With Notes and Exercises. W. Macpherson, M.A.

English Prose—A Book of Comparative Prose. Being Typical Essays arranged for Comparative Study. With Notes and Exercises. W. Macpherson, M.A.

KEATS — **Select Poems.** Isabella, Hyperion, The Eve of St. Agnes, Lamia. J. H. Boardman, B.A.

LAMB—**Select Tales from Shakspeare.** D. Frew, B.A.

LONGFELLOW—**Hiawatha.**

MACAULAY—**Essay on William Pitt the Younger.** W. Keith Leask, M.A.

Life of Johnson. John Downie.

Lays of Ancient Rome, with Ivry, The Armada, and Naseby.

MILTON—**Comus.** E. A. Phillips, B.A.

Samson Agonistes. E. K. Chambers, C.B., B.A., D.Litt.

Paradise Lost. Books I and II. F. Gorse, M.A.

POPE—**Rape of the Lock.** Frederick Ryland, M.A

Principles of Prose—The Principles of English Prose as Expressed by Great Writers. Collected by George L. Tarpley.

SCOTT—**The Lady of the Lake.** W. Keith Leask, M.A.

Marmion.

The Lay of the Last Minstrel.

Lord of the Isles. W. Keith Leask.

Three Stories from Scott. J. G. Fyfe, M.A.

Short Stories of the Nineteenth Century. J. G. Fyfe, M.A.

Short Stories of the Sea. J. G. Fyfe, M.A.

Some Strange Stories. J. G. Fyfe, M.A. (No Notes.)

TENNYSON—**The Princess.** Miss Edith Fry, M.A.

Cloth limp. Price 1s. each

ADDISON—**Sir Roger de Coverley.** Selected from the *Spectator*. Frances Wilcroft.

BLAKE—**Songs of Innocence and of Experience.** Arthur D. Innes, M.A.

BYRON—**Childe Harold's Pilgrimage.** Cantos II and III. John Downie, M.A.

Child Harold's Pilgrimage. Canto IV. David Frew, B.A.

CAMPBELL—**The Pleasures of Hope.** W. Keith Leask, M.A., and G. H. Ely, B.A.

The English Country Gentleman in Literature. Guy N. Pocock, M.A. (No Notes.)

GOLDSMITH—**She Stoops to Conquer.** H. Littledale, M.A., Litt.D.

The Good-natured Man. H. Littledale, M.A., Litt.D.

LONGFELLOW—**The Courtship of Miles Standish.** Rev. Henry Evans, D.D.

MILTON—**Paradise Lost.** Book I. F. Gorse, M.A.

Paradise Lost. Book II. F. Gorse.

Paradise Lost. Book III. F. Gorse.

Paradise Lost. Book IV. A. E. Roberts, M.A.

Paradise Lost. Book V. A. E. Roberts, M.A.

Paradise Lost. Book VI. A. E. Roberts, M.A.

Nativity Ode, L'Allegro, Il Penseroso, and **Lycidas.** Mary Olivia Kennedy, B.A.

PLUTARCH—**Lives of Solon and Nicias.** R. F. Patterson, M.A., D.Litt.

SHERIDAN—**The Critic.** R. F. Patterson, M.A., D.Litt.

Paper covers. Price 9d. each

BYRON—**Childe Harold's Pilgrimage.** Canto IV. David Frew, B.A.

TENNYSON—**The Coming of Arthur,** and **The Passing of Arthur.** David Frew, B.A.

BLACKIE & SON, LTD., 50 OLD BAILEY, LONDON

Printed in Great Britain by Blackie & Son, Ltd., Glasgow